THE GOD QUESTION AND MODERN MAN

THE GOD QUESTION
AND
MODERN MAN

by

HANS URS VON BALTHASAR

Foreword by John Macquarrie

THE SEABURY PRESS
NEW YORK

This translation from the original German, *Die Gottesfrage des Heutigen Menschen*
(Verlag Herold, Vienna and Munich), was made by

HILDA GRAEF

First Seabury Paperback *edition published 1967*

The God Question and Modern Man was originally published in 1958 under the
title *Science, Religion, and Christianity* by Newman Press, Westminster, Md.,
and Burns, Oates & Washbourne, London, and carried the notice—*Imprimatur:*
E. Morrogh Bernard, Vicarius Generalis Westmonasterii: die vi Maii MCMLVIII.

CONTENTS

AUTHOR'S NOTE

THIS ESSAY, which has grown out of lectures, is yet only fragmentary. A philosopher of culture and a historian might have amply orchestrated the theme, whereas I remain painfully conscious of the poverty of my documentation. But, being a theologian, I am concerned only with its Christian aspect, with its relation to the one thing necessary.

An understandable uneasiness prevented me from dedicating these pages to those martyrs of unity, the august army of the humiliated men of our atrocious time: to those who have been tortured, gassed, vivisected; to those deported and frozen to death in open cattle-trucks, to those kicked in the face by Nazi jackboots; to those deliberately forgotten ones who have given all in vain. *Ave caput cruentatum.*

FOREWORD by John Macquarrie

DURING the past few years, Roman Catholic theology has been experiencing a remarkable renewal and revitalization, and some of the most valuable contributions have come from Dr. Hans Urs von Balthasar. Born at Lucerne on August 12, 1905, he belongs to a family that has been well-known in the cultural and political life of Switzerland for generations.

Dr. Urs von Balthasar's student days were spent in some of the great European centers of learning. He studied first in the universities of Vienna, Berlin, and Zurich; and his interest at that time lay chiefly in philosophy. Then theology claimed his attention, and he went on to study it in the universities of Munich and Lyons. Since 1940 he has lived mainly in Basel, occupied largely in writing but giving time also to the service of the student community.

The number of his writings is very great, and their scope extends far beyond theology to such areas as literature, culture, history, and the spiritual life. The work presented in this volume has been translated into English by Hilda Graef, and was first published in 1958 as *Die Gottesfrage des Heutigen Menschen*. It is an excellent example of the way in which the author relates his theological thought to the many concerns of contemporary secular culture, and shows his extraordinarily sensitive grasp of these concerns. Among other works by Dr. Urs von Balthasar are a masterly study of his great compatriot Karl Barth (1951); a book on the Jewish philosopher Martin Buber (1958); and a volume on the theology of history (1959).

I believe that this translation of Dr. Urs von Balthasar's book on the question of God can offer an important contribution to the debates on this theme that have been going on in the English-speaking countries in the past few years. This book offers us an opportunity to see the question in a different light, and to hear a fresh voice that speaks out of a different cultural tradition from that which has been dominant in the debates up till now. This book cannot fail to bring new dimensions and, I venture to say, new depth to the discussions.

Let me mention a few reasons for hoping that this may be the case.

The first is the author's extraordinary mastery of the intellectual history of the West. Dr. Urs von Balthasar speaks modestly of the "fragmentary" character of his work and of the "poverty" of his documentation, but I know of no recent work by any English-speaking author that even approaches this book in the depth of its analysis or in its understanding of the infinitely complex factors—philosophical, literary, and political—that have gone into the fashioning of contemporary Western man. The trouble about the English-speaking debate is that much of it has been superficial and even journalistic. This Continental contribution puts contemporary man in the context of a long and painful development, some understanding of which is needed if this same contemporary man is to attain to a true self-understanding. But just because Dr. Urs von Balthasar has such an unusually wide understanding of this historical context, he has the wisdom not to make dogmatic generalizations either about the character of this history or about the kind of humanity to which it has led. The very complexity of history implies that it always has an ambiguous character. Whatever interpretation one places upon a historical event, another interpretation is always possible. There is always the temptation to present the half-truth as if it were the whole truth, especially if the half-truth in question has hitherto been neglected. I believe there has been a good deal of this kind of oversimplification (and thus of distortion) in recent debates on contemporary man, secularization, the idea of God, and the like, and Dr. Urs von Balthasar's book should remind us that the phenomena are immensely complex, and that even for one well versed in historical and contemporary currents of thought, these phenomena present ambiguities and seeming contradictions that are not easily resolved.

The next claim I want to make for this book is that, perhaps more than any other recent work on the subject, it is truly radical and realistic. It is truly radical because the author is willing to acknowledge not only the questionableness of the idea of God in our time, but the questionableness of some of the substitutes that get advocated in place of God. We are told perhaps that in place of God we should give our allegiance to Jesus or even to love. But for the man of today, these alternatives are hardly likely to be any more meaningful, for not only the word "God" but Christian language as a whole has deteriorated. Dr. Urs von Balthasar asks: "Must we really keep on using this word 'love,' which has gradually become unbearable, and continue to tear it to rags?" He is also clear that "the historical Jesus, such as we know him, cannot be brought into line with the modern humanitarian ideal."

In fact, he recognizes that the reconstruction of Christian theology is a more radical and more difficult business than that of discarding some elements (such as "God") and placing the emphasis on others (such as "love" or "Jesus"). These three stand or fall together. Without "God," "love" and "Jesus" lose their Christian significance and become trivialized, as has indeed largely happened already; while on the other hand, the Christian is not interested in any "God" apart from "Jesus" and "love." This radical approach of Dr. Urs von Balthasar is also realistic. It recognizes that Christian theology, as a historical phenomenon, cannot discard its history. Every historical movement is already in a situation and does not begin from scratch, as it were. If we are to go on talking about Christianity at all, we have to stand in continuity with the mainstream of the Christian tradition. This lays truly difficult and radical tasks of rethinking upon the theologian, but these are demanded by the historical situation.

A third reason for welcoming Dr. Urs von Balthasar's book is its genuinely Catholic outlook. I am using the word "Catholic" here in the most inclusive sense. I mean that our author speaks from the fullness of the Christian faith and tradition, rather than from some sectarian point of view. When he tells us, for instance, that God is concerned with the salvation of the world, not of the Church, and that one cannot draw a rigid boundary between the Church and humanity as a whole, we recognize that breadth of concern (call it a "universalism" if you will) that has found expression from the early Christian fathers on.

Unfortunately, the debates about God in the English-speaking countries have in the recent period been carried on almost entirely by Anglo-Saxon Protestants. No doubt Anglo-Saxon Protestants have some estimable virtues, but they also suffer from some very severe limitations. They came into being through protest, and protest always involves exaggeration and a one-sided point of view. It seems to me that Dr. Urs von Balthasar has been able to treat such questions as the problem of God and the nature of secularity in a far more balanced and dialectical way than can be found among Protestant writers of the Anglo-Saxon world. According to our author, what he calls "the whole world of sects and congregational churches of the Anglo-Saxon civilization" is much more easily "absorbed by the world" than is Catholic Christianity. Of course, if Christianity is merely absorbed by the world, it no longer has anything to say to the world or any role to play in it. This danger is already apparent in those Protestant writers who have gone to the extremes of "world-affirmation" and of uncritical acceptance of the methods, goals, and standards of contemporary culture.

This exaggerated desire to conform to the world may be seen as a violent reaction against opposing exaggerations of the past. Protestant theology, from Calvin to Barth, has despised natural theology and depreciated natural law; it has minimized human achievements, and sometimes even taught a doctrine of "total depravity"; it has sharply distinguished between "church" and "world," and has sometimes taught that God cares only for the "elect." It is not surprising that at last there should come a recoil against such distortions, and that this recoil should push some people to new extremes on the opposite side.

By contrast, Catholic theology has always had a more positive attitude to the world. It has found a place for natural religion, natural theology, natural law, and recognized their continuity with the Christian revelation. It has left something for man to do in cooperating with God in the work of salvation. An index of its attitude is perhaps to be seen in the way in which it has encouraged the arts and related them to its worship.

Because Catholic theology has never been entirely negative toward the "world," it is not now pushed to an uncritical affirmation of the "wordly" mentality, but is able to maintain a dialectic. This comes out very clearly in Dr. Urs von Balthasar's remarks on secularization. He welcomes the positive aspects of this process and the opportunities which it affords for the betterment of human life. But he is not so naïve as to be blind to its demonic possibilities. He sees it also as defection, and if there is much to be affirmed in contemporary civilization, there is also much that must, from a Christian point of view, be judged as vulgar, cruel, and mindless.

Mention of "secularization" suggests that we should look more closely at this expression. The word "secular" has been appearing prominently in much recent theological discussion, but it is a word with several meanings, and confusion arises when these are not properly sorted out. For instance, Ronald Gregor Smith, Harvey Cox, and Paul Van Buren present us with three fairly distinct, though related, concepts of the secular. Of these three Protestant writers, it is Ronald Gregor Smith's idea of the secular that perhaps comes closest to Dr. Urs von Balthasar's; though I am inclined to think that it is Paul Van Buren who stays closest to ordinary English usage.

There seem to be two major strands in Dr. Urs von Balthasar's concept of the secular. One of these is the familiar theme of the stripping away from Nature of every vestige of animism. As understood by modern science and as exploited by technology, the world has no longer any pretensions to a divine or sacred character. It is below man, not above him, and it is increasingly brought under his control. The last strongholds of the romantics are falling before the universal thrust of a profane science and technology. It is clear to both believer and unbeliever alike, says our author, that the world is not God. Even the ends of the earth, once thought to merge into the heavenly regions, have come near; the mystery has been dissolved, and our lives are set in a secular universe.

The second strand has to do with the way in which man has come to understand himself in this environment. No longer does he understand himself as a divine spark that has somehow got lost in a world of matter, or as an angelic being that has strayed from the realm of pure spirit, or even as the thinking subject of idealist philosophy. He is in solidarity with the cosmos that has brought him forth. He accepts his total existence as a being-in-the-world. His body is not an appendage to his true self, but a constituent part of it, necessary for the attainment of personal being. Thus, secularity is understood in terms of man's being-in-the-world as well as in terms of the world's de-divinization.

As a consequence of these developments, the center of interest in philosophy has shifted from cosmology to anthropology. Since the world is below man, we cannot understand man as part of the world. On the other hand, since the world has brought forth man, who now in turn increasingly shapes and controls the world, our understanding of the world must be reached through an understanding of man. This demands the development of new categories for the construction of a philosophy of personal being, for such categories were lacking or only rudimentary in the traditional cosmological philosophies.

What then are we to say of man? Dr. Urs von Balthasar is quite clear that just as the world is not God, man is not God either. "Man has transcended things; they can no longer be God for him. He has come to know himself sufficiently to have no more desire to worship himself." With these words, our author dissociates himself from atheistic humanism, for which man is the measure of all things.

The point about man, who has transcended Nature, is that
he is not himself another "nature" complete and self-contained, but that his "nature" (if we can call it such) is always
open. This openness of man is a recurring theme of the book.
It is an openness to futurity and transcendence, and it is here
that the question of God arises for modern man. We might
say that if Dr. Urs von Balthasar has a "natural" theology, it
is based not on Nature in the physical and biological sense,
but on the open and self-transcending "nature" of man. God
has been driven out of the natural world by the advance of
science, and has retired into his mysterious transcendence.
Man, too, in the openness of his "nature," knows a dimension
of mystery and transcendence. It is there that he experiences
grace and judgment, and hears the word addressed to him,
the word he assigns to the mystery he calls "God." If the end
of the old conceptions of God has been interpreted by some
as the triumph of atheism, it is taken by our author as herald-
ing the birth of a deeper understanding of God. "A growing
vagueness and transcendence of the concept of God may be
but a symptom indicating that this concept itself is growing
among men." On the other hand, the emergence of modern
atheism is a rebuke to the Church for its failure to hold fast
and teach a genuinely biblical and Christian idea of God.

Man is not God, but it is in and through man that God
comes to us. Indeed, the central assertion of the Christian
faith is that God was made man. One of the finest sections of
this book is the concluding one, entitled "The Sacrament of
the Brother." It is in the whole realm of personal relations
that God becomes real to us. He is no abstraction, but a concrete Reality. But again, Dr. Urs von Balthasar makes it
clear that what he has in mind is more than an exalted humanitarianism, and certainly that "God" is much more than just
a fancy name for humanity. Rather, it is the transcendent
God who makes a right human relation possible. "The adventure of losing self will not be worthwhile if I do not meet
God in my brother, if no breath of infinity stirs in this love,
if I cannot love my brother with a love that comes from a

higher source than my finite capacity of loving; in short, if what in our meeting may bear the sublime name of love does not come from God and return to him."

Every book on these difficult themes leaves unanswered problems and is open at points to critical questions. Dr. Urs von Balthasar makes the momentous assertion that the meeting between persons is the norm of all knowledge and should be basic to a theory of knowledge. This thesis is central to the book, but it needs to be more fully explicated and established, and its scope more precisely delimited. Again, the author, while showing an openness to the non-Christian religions and while frankly acknowledging that Christianity, whether its adherents like it or not, is itself a religion, sometimes appears unsympathetic to non-Christian faiths, especially when he speaks of the religions of Asia. Some of the judgments of the book are bound to be questioned. Is the author fair to Dante, in stressing the cosmological aspects of Dante's thinking while apparently overlooking its very definite existential dimensions? Or is he fair to his fellow citizen at Basel, Karl Jaspers, who writes after all as one concerned with the philosophical foundations of the possibility of faith, rather than as the exponent of a particular concrete faith?

I mention these questions, and I could mention others, simply to indicate that although I have praised this book highly, I do not suggest for a moment that it ends the discussion. Its virtue is precisely that it carries the discussion further and, I believe, points us in the right direction. I have every hope that it will make a solid and important contribution to the fundamental theological debates now going on in the English-speaking countries.

INTRODUCTION

SCIENCE[1] can be defined only from the point of view of man. It is the activity of *homo sapiens*, who thus becomes also *homo faber*, because he masters life and things in the way he has previously apprehended them. This connexion has existed as long as there have been men; nevertheless, it becomes increasingly important as civilization progresses. For man tends to leave things less and less to the course of nature, but increasingly subjects the conditions of life, including even his own most hidden and intimate concerns, to investigation, and so to practical reason. In this sense science is bound up with man's nature as such, yet is highly differentiated in the course of history. Being a human phenomenon, science is in principle accessible to every man. If a scientific insight is too deep or too high for an individual, it is so only for accidental reasons. This remains valid even for that hierarchy of knowledge whose higher stages demand a more deeply moral and existential "engagement" of the whole personality, as is the case in the terminal science of philosophy. A certain esoteric quality of knowledge does not exclude its being related to "man as such"; for the full realization of his powers depends closely on his historical context.

Christianity, on the other hand, must be examined primarily in its historical aspect. It cannot be derived from the nature of man; considered in the way its historical sources as well as its representatives invariably present it, it is a phenomenon that rests wholly on the historical fact of the appearance of Christ. This includes his life and death, his self-interpretation in word and existence, and finally his resurrection from the dead, confirmed by trustworthy witnesses. A non-Christian, it is true, may afterwards criticize this phenomenon from outside, that is to say from the human and scientific point of view. Nevertheless, in order to

[1] *Wissenschaft*, i.e. science in a wider sense, comprising all branches of learning. (Tr.)

grasp the essence of Christianity, one will first have to consider what it says about itself. Its basis is then seen to be the existence and self-revelation of Christ as the God-man and Saviour, hence trusting faith in him is the organ that mediates the knowledge of this truth.

What a Christian is cannot be derived *a priori*—just as little as what Jesus Christ is. Starting with what he has done and said about himself, we must ask at once what kind of men he addressed and claimed for his own, what kind of men were the apostles, and what Christ made of a Paul or a John and, finally, of all the typical representatives of the Christian life, whether personally or "through the power of his idea". We may also critically consider the masses that are still affected indirectly by Christianity without being existentially open and surrendered to the "idea" of Jesus Christ. We shall, indeed, be justified in doing this, but only in so far as it be admitted that this sociological problem is the result of being estranged from the centre of Christian truth, and this, in its turn, is a Christian problem.

What Christ is and confers does not pertain to human nature as such, because it is the divine word, truth and life; hence the essence of Christianity and its truth, however experienced, is realized wherever a man becomes aware of the existence of Christ as the Word or the Father in such a way that he will fall down and adore, following the Johannine way of light that leads to a glimpse of the Absolute. ("I am he who am speaking with thee", John 4.26.)[1] At this moment the utterly free self-revelation of God in Christ meets man's utterly free decision to open and surrender himself to truth, though this has been made by human freedom under the influence of divine revelation. In St John's Gospel this ultimate flash of revelation is normally preceded by long discussions on the subject of truth, by which the human mind is slowly led and prepared to make the act of faith. The *praeambula fidei* are seen in the light of preparing and helping grace which suddenly and peremptorily demands belief, precisely because of this rational preparation and not without it. Christian truth offered to a public that is not yet believing but more or less searching, is meant to lead to a sudden meeting, in which a man

[1] cf. *Ibid.* 1. 34, 39, 48-51; 2. 11; 6. 20, 51f.; 9. 37; 11. 25; 20. 28 *et freq.*

will be gained for the Truth, fall down and confess: "My Lord and my God." Anyone incapable of making this act has no right to call himself a Christian merely because of certain values and views taken over from the preparatory stage, nor has he any qualification to discuss Christianity with authority. It is true that Christianity claims to be universal, since salvation is meant for all, and hence interior grace is offered to men even beyond the frontiers of visible graces. Nevertheless, while granting this, we may yet never by-pass the unique historical personality of Jesus, on whose actual existence—a promise that has been fulfilled—depends the universal validity of Christian truth for all mankind.

Thus described, the two spheres of scholarship and Christianity seem to have scarcely any connexion. For the former produces a universal human culture, whereas the latter always bases its possible claim to universality on a personal decision for a truth which is independent of human nature, and so is bound to be questionable, even scandalous, from the purely human point of view. Here we ought perhaps to mention the apparent indifference of the founder of the Christian religion to cultural values and achievements. In his sermons and parables, as well as in his way of life that might almost be called nomadic, he always refers to the simplest and most natural human conditions and is without care for the morrow, an attitude which he wishes his disciples to share. We might add the eschatological outlook of the first generation of Christians and, springing from this, their evident indifference to worldly scholarship and culture. Even when St Augustine was writing his *Confessions* it was still the fashion among Christians to speak of "a certain Cicero".[1] In view of this, it might be urged that the subsequent influence and leadership of Christianity in the domain of culture was alien to its nature, and that it ought to abandon all scholarly concerns.

On the other hand, the relationship between the two spheres is evidently not one of complete separation, the natural as opposed to the supernatural. However we may draw up the frontiers between them, it is clear that they both enter the field of *Weltanschauung* and religion. As a matter of history, Christianity, whether it likes it or not, is one religion among others, and it

[1] *Conf.* III, 4.

acknowledged this fact at a very early stage by fixing its own place among the religions. For it attempted to represent not only Judaism but also the pagan religions as a "preparation for the Gospel", an historical road directed by providence towards its own centre and summit. On the other hand, if we consider more deeply how scholarship is possible and on what it is founded, we shall realize at once that it is in any case based on a view of the whole, a *Weltanschauung*—and this, again, is indisputable. It is naïve to imagine that in any sphere of human knowledge there could be something like a photographic reproduction of reality without the interpreting, and thus the selecting, emphasizing and omitting, function of reason. Yet this view emerges time and again, though it is usually soon discarded as a chimera by the wise, not only among philosophers, but even among scholars and scientists. The world may be considered in various aspects, such as nature or history, the external or the internal, the subhuman or the human order, the physical or the psychical realm. Yet always it appears under the aspect of being and hence needs interpretation by reason, which thus proves to be a function which not only passively reproduces, but actively considers and judges (*intellectus agens, dividens et componens*). A special science is therefore needed to watch, examine and justify this activity, and this is philosophy. Philosophy discovers the presuppositions of that function of reason which considers the nature of universal being. From this latter there arises the idea of the absolute or divine Being, and thus philosophy necessarily borders on religion. It may even be equated, in its reach, with the intellectual side of religion or, what amounts to the same, with "natural" theology. Thus science attains at least the boundary beyond which lies the Christian revelation. However much the human mind may need the assistance of purifying and elevating grace in order actually to assent to the Word of God in faith, this act presupposes the capacity of listening and openness to the absolute.

Thus the circle is closed. What had before been unrelated, are now brought into a connexion, merely possible and accidental, but necessary. Even a superficial glance at the intellectual history of mankind suffices to confirm this fact: Christianity not only formed and penetrated philosophy like a leaven, but with its help powerfully influenced all departments of culture and scholarship. The existing *Weltanschauung*, the "world-view" of antiquity, is taken over as the framework within which the Christian penetration of the world and the apostolate to all nations and times are to be realized. This framework was criticized only in so far as its concrete forms seemed to be incompatible with the Christian message. For the rest, it was left unchanged for the duration of its historical validity; indeed, it was vigorously used to make the transcendent Christian truth palatable and intelligible to men: for, after all, in the first instance truth can only be proclaimed in terms of the most universal ideas about being and the world. Precisely because it was mediated in this form, Christianity became a major power forming history and civilization. Throughout the centuries of "Christendom" the Christian view of the world and of man continued to decide the way in which reason should conduct its enquiries, and conditions were shaped in accordance with these questions and answers. Whether it was a question of planning a state or of building a city and deciding the place of the church in it, whether men were concerned with the function of art in this latter or with the right use of human language and its possibilities: everything was seen with "Christian eyes" and arranged accordingly, notwithstanding its relative autonomy. To take an example, we need only consider the influence which a purely Christian theological interpretation of history such as St Augustine's *City of God* exercised on the whole pragmatic historical science of the Middle Ages and even far beyond.

It may be objected that this marriage between Christianity and culture rested on a unique and transitory natural situation whose causes historical science has unequivocally established. Further, that its historical hour is either already past or nearly over, since the centuries of transition to our own time have clearly shown an increasing tendency to separate Church and State, faith and knowledge, theology and secular science, in fact towards divorcing grace and nature, which in the Middle Ages had been entangled and interwoven with each other. This tendency is clearly seen in the disaster of the Reformation, by which Christianity ceased to be an all-embracing spiritual and secular home. Henceforth the Churches confront each other as clear-cut "denominations" which, despite their inner oppositions, have to live together in the secular sphere and hence are normally tolerant enough to leave the choice between them to the individual. This is all the more necessary since this individual increasingly develops into a non-Christian on whom even for external reasons the denominations can no longer exercise any pressure. This holds good not only for Protestantism, at the basis of whose doctrinal teaching is the divorce between the natural world and community on the one hand, and the invisible personal "interiority" and decision of faith on the other. The compulsory acceptance of this enforced situation has also become largely inevitable for Catholics, who find such a separation of spheres far less congenial, since they regard the Church as essentially visible and its apostolate as extending to all secular spheres. Consequently the neo-scholastics have been concerned to work out a clear-cut distinction between faith and knowledge and between Church and State with their proper methods and competences. For, according to the Vatican Council, both differ in their principle of knowledge as well as their subject[1] and, proceeding according to their proper principles and method,[2] meet only in their borderland, even though their common origin in God and their common hierarchy of values exclude on principle any real opposition.

As opposed to the strong medieval tendency to unite the spheres, their clear separation is without doubt an expression of the modern situation, which should on no account be viewed as something merely to be deplored, as has been stated in ecclesiastical circles. For this separation guarantees not only the freedom of the Church, which had formerly always been threatened, and has now at last been made possible; it also clearly emphasizes the transcendence of revelation as opposed to all merely philosophical interpretation of the world: "For the doctrine of faith which God has revealed is not proposed to human perspicacity to be developed by it like a philosophical tenet, but is transmitted to the Bride of Christ as a divine deposit to be faithfully preserved and infallibly interpreted."[3] This teaching is of course entirely different from the liberal divorce that has become the custom under the influence of Max Weber, who has, however, been widely misunderstood.

[1]Denzinger, 1795.   [2]*Ibid.*, 1799.   [3]*Ibid.*, 1800.

According to this view, science forms the social and political human sphere, for which it alone is theoretically and practically valid, owing to an objectivity that can be proved by reason; whereas the "religious *Weltanschauung*" presupposes a personal and subjectively interior decision which only the individual can make, and which he must justify before his own conscience. The Catholic Church will always repudiate this antithesis. She claims that her faith rests on objective foundations and demands that her competence in all questions of civic and public life should be recognized in as far as they are affected by her doctrine. Nevertheless, a formal similarity will not be disputed, since both interpretations start from an existing dualistic situation. For the idea of the individual (and thus the importance of his freedom and decision) must gain an increasing importance also for the Church, since she is essentially a community, as opposed to a merely social mass civilization. Finally, medieval philosophy, closely united with metaphysics, claimed to supply the fundamental principles of the underlying individual sciences in one solid system of thought, a claim which in the contemporary situation can no longer be upheld in the same way.

Yet, even now, the present "dualistic" interpretation is opposed by a new line of thought which, going back to the preceding "monistic" one, seems destined to supplant the development we have just outlined. This is the simple realization, brought about by the spiritual and historical situation of modern man, that there is no such thing as the liberal dream of complete scientific objectivity. This is impossible not only practically, but, as has been shown before, theoretically. In fact, mankind has known increasingly frightful catastrophes and is now hovering on the brink of destruction, because science and the technical knowledge based on it have been pursued without adequate personal responsibility. Men are beginning to understand that the liberal's apparent suspense of decision was a decision of the gravest consequences, hence that there is no such thing as pure objectivity. Indeed, the most "objective" are those who seek to regulate the course of events by their interpretation of themselves and the world, and their resulting responsibility. To do this is vitally urgent; if neglected, if postponed unduly, a choice may no longer be possible.

This warning has never before been so necessary, because the danger had never approached so closely. It arises now from the whole situation of mankind, and man is urged to remain within a tradition that has always been the foundation of all human civilization and whose rôle as such only the most recent generations have failed to acknowledge.

Western civilization is a sufficient example. Its fundamental idea at each stage of its development has always consisted in a conscious blending of science and its application, on the one hand, with philosophy and religion on the other. *Homo faber* has always received his authorization from *Homo sapiens*. From Plato onwards the highest type of man has been the philosopher-king, who, from the heights of contemplation, perceives the whole meaning of existence and so is able to co-ordinate the various spheres of intellectual and physical work. The ordered systems that Greece and Rome gave to the world existed ultimately in the light of this idea. Christianity took it over and, through St Augustine, developed it in the Middle Ages. Bonaventure's *Reductio artium*, St Thomas's *Summa* and Dante's *De monarchia* are representatives of this general trend. Even the modern scientific cosmologies are constantly accompanied by a religious philosophy which, carefully noting all the changes in the world picture, never abandons its normative function. The same may be said of Neo-Platonic cosmic mysticism in its application by Nicholas of Cusa, the Florentines, Bruno and Kepler. It was even more evident in the powerful and almost violent union of science and religion, mathematics (or "geometry") and mysticism in the dynamic cosmology of Leibniz and the monistic system of Spinoza, as well as in that of Pascal which, though personal, always envisages the same unity. They were all meant, each in its own way, to halt the schism between the secular and the spiritual spheres that had originated in the Reformation. Kant's philosophy unfortunately sanctioned this dualism in large measure; yet it is the inmost meaning and the merit of the most powerful intellectual movement of modern times, German Idealism, in the classical and romantic periods, that it desired to heal this schism by every means in its power. Fichte's frequently revised *Wissenschaftslehre*, which aimed at rooting all science and technology in a comprehensive philosophy of the freely deciding ego, is the heir of the tradition that stems from Plato's *Republic*. Schleiermacher's first work, *On Religion*, develops the thesis that neither scholarship nor culture nor morality is possible without religion. Indeed, the opposition between classicism and romanticism is not deep enough to prevent them from completely agreeing on the spiritual and secular unity of man and his culture. Hegel ordered the *a priori* structures of all individual sciences within a philosophy systematically and historically developed, and Schelling in his old age gathered all forms of human religion (which foreshadow the various civilizations) into the womb of revelation.

Nor can it be denied that a universal conception of man, life and nature was offered also by the more robust nineteenth-century schools of thought, e.g. by Feuerbach changing Hegelianism into a purely anthropological concept, and by materialism and evolutionism. These systems acknowledged the scientific activity of the time as necessary and indispensable, and gave to it concrete directions for its research. Even the modern existentialist trend in philosophy has by no means resigned the claim to interpret man as a whole within the world as well as his position at the present time. Otherwise Heidegger and Jaspers, each with his own idea of the "catholicity of reason", would not react so violently against all those activities that derive from the absolute claims of individual sciences and threaten to narrow, endanger and destroy the idea of man in his universality. It is precisely these two thinkers who have approached closely to the religious source of philosophy, giving expression to those depths of the spirit where philosophy meets ethics and aesthetics (cf. Heidegger's interpretation of Hölderlin). This should prove conclusively that despite all structural changes of our thought we have not cut loose from the sources of our spiritual tradition. Hence it is only reasonable to continue the work begun by Augustine (in Neo-Platonism) and Aquinas (in Aristotelianism) and to express in modern idiom the Christian revelation which, humanly speaking, would perish if it were completely isolated from the profane world. These great examples clearly show that this cannot be done without separating the valuable from the worthless in philosophy; but they show equally that the work is possible and indeed necessary, both for the continuation of Christianity in the cultural sphere as well as for the capacity of culture to be at all influenced and shaped by Christianity.

Several results follow from all this. First, the two realities of science and Christianity, though seemingly unconnected, are nevertheless related by an intermediate sphere. From the scholar's point of view this appears as *Weltanschauung*, from the Christian's as "religion", and from the centre as philosophy, remaining a unity in all these aspects. Further, in the course of history the extremes of science and Christianity tend undeniably to separate and become autonomous. Yet modern man realizes the urgent demand not to sever science from *Weltanschauung* and religion, because these are the ground from which all human action and decision springs and is justified.

Hence, though the fundamental formal relations between science, philosophy and Christianity are unalterable, their concrete connexions are subject to a law of changing phases and nuances. History reveals the various aspects of the one human nature, and through these changing aspects the one and objectively uniform revelation of Christ can present itself in new shades of its interior richness. The question might be asked which is the deeper and primary factor in this law of change: is it the shifting of phases due to natural, historical and cultural developments—in which case those truths of revelation that have so far remained in obscurity but are now brought to the light would appear as an answer to the changed secular situation; or is it a mysterious, supernatural law of the Holy Spirit who, directing the Church, gradually uncovers the secret depths of the revelation of Christ, and therefore induces the necessary development of maturity in profane history? In view of the inextricable entanglement of the natural with the supernatural in human history, this problem remains insoluble. What may appear as the cause if viewed from one angle, may be seen as an effect from another. It is enough to realize the close interplay of both elements and thus sense that the world is directed by the one divine Providence. Nevertheless, if we investigate the laws governing the change of phases, we must always bear in mind that the changes that can be stated are on the side of human history: here decisions are constantly made, here civilizations mature and wither away, here discoveries are made that determine the future.

Compared with this colourful sphere of history the Church at first seems almost lifeless. It is her vocation to remain what she has been from the beginning; if only she actually is what she is meant to be, she has no need to grow in any relevant dimension in order to become herself. Neither is this character changed by her calling to be a light radiating to all nations and times, for it is determined not by an historical lack of life and energy, but by the matchless eschatological "fullness of Christ", which is at her disposal and which, according to St Paul, she mysteriously is herself.

The line we have to follow in our investigation results immediately from this consideration. The world of modern science is little concerned with the content of the Christian revelation. But if it does show interest in it, this is so narrowly confined to the needs of the world and of civilization that it is very uncertain if such an attitude is at all capable of grasping what is specifically Christian. The world, however, that is marked by modern science, is interested in *Weltanschauung*, philosophy and religion, because it seeks to interpret its own meaning. Indeed, the very fact that science and technology ask their own questions on the meaning and order of existence is itself part of the intellectual situation. Hence the object of the first part must be the relation between science and religion. Now this should be cleared up even to those recesses where a man must needs become a question to himself, inasmuch as at the same time and in a quite elemental way he is entirely open to the whole and is also compelled to understand and decide at once and absolutely. Hence he will simply have to pay attention to the only religion that shows and promises him something other than an echo of his own being from the cosmos, or an elongation of his own being into the cosmos. This is the Word of God which, against all hope and expectation, offers him both at the same time: that which cannot be derived from anything at all, because it is not contained in the natural being of man, and the perfection of this human being from within, since the Word of God becomes nothing else, nothing less than—Man. Thus in the second part we shall have to treat of religion and Christianity.

I

SCIENCE AND RELIGION

A. THE WAY TO ANTHROPOLOGY

As LONG AS man has been living on earth there has been spirit, and thus knowledge and "scholarship", hence also culture and technical achievement. This is proved by the first stone axe, the first fire, the first funeral. And as far as human tradition can be traced back—and possibly the farther back the more evident it becomes—man has always been a religious being; he knows that he is subject to a divine power which he must recognize and honour, and from which he is to expect salvation. There is thus through all historical changes a permanently fixed plan of human existence, a perennial humanity.

The factor most deeply affected by change in the great phases of the development of mankind is man's relation to nature. The law of development can roughly be described according to the three stages of Auguste Comte, provided Comte's own superficial description is dropped and the phases are made to occur within the comprehensive idea of perennial humanity. This would then mean that each phase is a different presentation and "potency" of the whole human being: of his being spirit within nature, of his governing attitude towards the surrounding world, and of his religious relation to the Deity. Now, it is possible that each phase possesses a validity which is not simply taken over and absorbed by the next. Even if a "progress" from the earlier to the later phase can be affirmed, this is not the whole sense of the change; rather, values of expression (*Ausdruckswerte*) remain linked to a certain time; they are no longer possible in the following period that is differently construed, and hence need to be reverently and vividly remembered if man, who today can no longer be what he once was, is to retain his own wholeness. Now the thesis of this investigation is already taking shape: if the law of "change as progress" is the development of the idea of man in the world, if therefore philosophy will ever more clearly find its centre and form in a total anthropology, this must always go together with humanity's growing consciousness of its own history, which retains in a living memory even what it once was but can be no longer, just as a man cannot reach total maturity without a living memory of his youth.

The primitive view of the world is characterized by a semi-religious relation of man to nature bearing magic, animistic and totemistic traits. This will have been fundamentally outgrown when the mind becomes conscious of itself in the great religions, and philosophy comes into existence. Yet it will survive in a way, because even in this second, philosophical period, the cosmos will retain certain divine features, from classical Greece to the Areopagite, and down to the Renaissance and German classicism and romanticism. The second and third periods overlap in a similar way. According to Comte, these bear the names of philosophy and science, of considering nature and of mastering it. For in a period when the attitude to nature becomes increasingly technical we are neither able nor willing to give up the philosophical attitude to the world, though—and here progress is most evident—the third, technical attitude is no longer compatible with the first, religio-magical one.

Man realizes that this gain implies loss; and Comte was not unaware of this. When knowledge and science, and hence also practical behaviour, are increasingly differentiated, a certain simple view of the world will have to cede to a very complicated and specialized picture of it. From now on, things move in obedience to the call of the human mind, and this fact becomes so important that the former primary fact appears to be forgotten and obliterated, namely that things, too, call out to man, who, obeying the call, comes into contact with the deeper forces of nature and uses them for his own advantage. There was already a certain loss when the magician was superseded by the philosopher, who is primarily a man who contemplates things and thus is detached from them. In general, when man became increasingly intellectualized, he lost the whole world of animal instincts, by which sub-human life communicates with itself and its surroundings.

Traces of this have still been preserved in specially endowed individuals who know how to read the nature-language of spirit, e.g. physiognomy in all its forms, palmistry, graphology, the art of sensing how a destiny is embedded in the whole planetary scheme (astrology), and all the variants of a divining medicine from the Tibetans to Paracelsus; and this does not exclude the possibility that the necessary subjective condition may be consistent with the fact that these arts follow objective and scientifically definable laws. At the end of the second period, the romantics once more attempted to salvage all this in a comprehensive philosophy of nature and spirit, just as they had tried to salvage the mythology of the first and second epochs in the third. It is here that human limitations become manifest: when the sun of the spirit has reached a certain height above the horizon of nature, those enchanting phenomena of sunrise, when light and atmosphere merge in an intoxicated union, become impossible. Perhaps something similar may happen once again at the sunset of human history—but no one can yet, even vaguely, foresee its course.

With the progress of the mind, nearness to and union with nature are inevitably lost. The loss of religion, though often wrongly equated with these, is far less. That the contrary should appear is due to the fact—amply supported by a wealth of documents and human experience—that in the first stage the relation to nature is indissolubly entangled with that to the Godhead. A numen is thought to inhabit the hitherto unknown forces of nature; this represents the central reality, whose functions, organs and spheres of influence are the individual living beings such as animals, plants, men and tribes. Priests and medicine men mediate the contact with the divinities present in nature; magic rites and formulae can reconcile the hostile powers and induce the friendly ones to serve men. The main concern of human life is to know how to be on good terms with the Deity. The dead return into the real world of numinous powers, whether their existence be continued in the lower sphere of nature, or whether, as in China and Egypt, they enter the world of the highest divinities that determine destiny: the living will always continue their contact with them and recommend themselves to them by honouring their memory. Hence it is only reasonable that sex and procreation should be introduced into the inmost sphere of the cosmic religious attitude; and thus ritual practice will be combined with orgiastic elements into one unified human mode of behaviour.

The magic attitude to the cosmos is superseded by the philosophical or contemplative one as soon as the world reveals itself to the awakening rational thought as governed no longer by arbitrary numinous powers but by unchangeable laws. Then a melody such as has never been heard before begins to sound: the meditative Hellenic mind, guided by Babylonian thought, discovers the harmony of the spheres. The image of reality such as it appears now will generally be accepted, despite all kinds of variations, until the time of Goethe. It is the picture of the cosmos which in its order represents the logos, the world-reason, and whose essence is mirrored in the microcosm of man. The variations of this theme are manifold indeed. They range from the objective and subjective idealisms to naturalism and materialism, and to those systems which include both nature and spirit. Nevertheless, the fundamental human attitude always rests on the contemplation of a paradigmatic order realized in the universe, and results in a mode of action that will reflect and realize what has been experienced in this contemplation.

As proof of this we would neither adduce the Platonic view, which was taken over by the Alexandrines and St Augustine and embodied in the early Middle Ages, nor even Aristotelianism, which St Thomas received from the Arabs. We would rather take Stoicism as our example. Since this was the most widely diffused form of higher and average education in later antiquity it infiltrated everywhere. In the West it continued to be the real inheritance of antiquity after, in the early Renaissance, the Platonic influence had ceased for the time being and the Aristotelian view of nature had been superseded by the modern functional one; hence it was at the basis of the cultural formation of the sixteenth, seventeenth and eighteenth centuries. Stoic influence is unmistakable in Erasmus and Thomas More, and is still more pronounced with Montaigne and his followers for whom Plutarch took the place of the Bible. It enters into the plays of Corneille and into La Rochefoucauld's and La Bruyère's view of man as well as into Spinoza's metaphysics and Fénelon's ethic of resignation. From there it floods the popular literature of the Enlightenment, but it also plays a part in the character-formation of the Jesuits, and we may not overlook the profound relationship between Ignatius himself and his teaching to "find God in all things" with Epictetus or the Cleanthes hymn. The fundamental tenet of this spiritual world, which may be interpreted pantheistically as well as panentheistically, is the identity of nature and reason. It asserts the analogy between the physical and spiritual, necessary and free, social and private; but it clearly gives the whole, the cosmos, priority over the part, that is man. At his best he is a spark from the central fire (*scintilla animae*), and he has to prove and actualize this nature of fire and spirit in accordance with his being. He must reflect the whole in himself, while submitting to its gently compelling law in harmony with which he preserves the parts given him for organic penetration.[1] The whole is the comprehensive world order, the macropolis, designed to be imitated not only by the human state (an aim constantly pursued by the Emperor Marcus Aurelius), but also by the individual human organism and spiritual "household". This is also at the root of the striking Classical-Christian simile of the world as a stage and a play in which every individual has his own part: all being identical in the spark of the soul, they differ only in costume. Calderon and the whole theatre of the Baroque once more represent this view; Schelling, too, interprets the world and providence in this way, and Goethe does the same by showing man's "theatrical mission" in his *Wilhelm Meister*.

The wise man whom Plato puts at the head of his state contemplates the order of the world; from calm contemplation of the heights the right action flows into the lower spheres of everyday life. The Greek depreciation of action is the natural counterpart of the curse Genesis pronounced on man's work and labour, a view shared by the Christians of antiquity to the time of Augustine and Gregory. The Greeks looked on contemplation as a means to transcend the transitory present and gaze into the world of eternal ideas; their Christian successors as a foretaste of future beatitude.

[1]Cf. the Greek *syn-terein*, i.e. preserve together, = *synderesis*, the principle of practical reason right up to the Scholastic period.

The place of magic was taken by *sophia* (wisdom); and whereas the former attributed ultimate reality to the numenal powers, the latter found it in the splendour of the world essence, radiating in the living and spiritual formation of the universe. True, the plan of the world and the ethical ideal vary according to the place of the central fire. The Stoics situate it in the centre of the world, whereas Plotinus locates it in the heights above it. Yet historically both views continually absorb or pass into each other, as is borne out by history from Scotus Erigena, Albert and Thomas, to Nicholas of Cusa, Bruno, Shaftesbury, Hemsterhuis and Goethe. The family likeness will be noticed at once. Even where God is seen to be transcendent, he is at the same time so immanent that the world is experienced and understood as a spontaneous revelation: the good is diffusive of itself. Cosmosophy passes immediately into theosophy, and all the more smoothly, since both in paganism and in Christianity the highest and noblest parts of the cosmos are thought to belong to the sphere of the divine, to the kingdom of God or to heaven. The "supra-celestial place" is the seat of the Deity and of the blessed souls and spirits; indeed, the predominant rôle of the gods in ancient, and of the angels in medieval thought between Dionysius and Thomas, should never be forgotten. And this *topos hyperouranios* remains in immediate contact with the cosmic sky and the celestial bodies and souls that are above earthly becoming and death.

Thus from Plato to Goethe the mood of man contemplating the God-indwelt universe is always one of cosmic enthusiasm. It may take the most diverse forms, from the Dionysian all-one intoxication to the most delicate religious and Christian emotion, as is evidenced by the Book of Wisdom and the first, Hellenic, part of Paul's speech on the Areopagus down to the citation from Aratus. But it can also be sensed in the ascensions of the austere poetry of Dante into the highest heavenly spheres of the cosmos, and certainly in Goethe's *Ganymede*. Despite the eschatological mood of late antiquity and the periodical apocalyptic upheavals at the beginning and end of the Middle Ages, the prevailing view is one of being sheltered in the all-embracing union of "God and nature" or "God or nature" (*Deus sive natura*). Indeed, this first conception of the close relationship of the cosmos with the divine

Logos permitted Christianity, as it developed, to interpret the incarnation of the Logos in Christ in a grandiose universalistic manner, from Justin and Origen to Baader and Solovyev. Yet we shall not fail to recognize here the organically surviving tradition of the first, magical and numinous, period despite its being thoroughly transformed. Inasmuch as the third period is particularly characterized by the elimination of this remainder of the first in the second epoch, the latter is proved to be a moment of transition in a unified development of man's idea of the cosmos.

Between the second and third phases, too, this development is so organic that it would be difficult to prove it by considering philosophy alone. But we see here a sharp turn towards a scientific attitude to the world both in theory and practice, and, closely connected with this, towards history as the last connexion between the history of nature and modern man. The turning point comes when the human mind, interrogating nature more closely and precisely by means of experiments, compels things to give more precise answers. Despite all detours and setbacks, the mathematical and technical domination of nature prevails and, having fought and repressed the former contemplative and religious attitude, finally comes to eliminate it entirely.

On one plane the battle is dramatically fought out between idealistic romanticism and modern matter-of-factness, whereas on another the change comes about quite painlessly and naturally: this happened in the sphere of philosophy, where from the beginning of the second period the formula of the macro- and the microcosm had a double meaning. It could be interpreted so that man was taken to be strictly a part and an image of the actual great cosmos; but it could also be taken in a way that the cosmos appeared as an elongation of man, its archetypal nucleus. Both views meet in the mythical idea of Adam Kadmon, the cosmic Man who, disintegrated in consequence of some Fall, was (in Manichaean and Cabbalistic myths) imprisoned in matter and so became the microcosm of empirical man. Thus anthropology has always been latent in cosmology; for if the cosmos is really thought of as a great harmony, it could only be interpreted after the pattern of human nature, as a balanced unity of the spiritual and the material (the first, being the form, governing the second), inner and outer, upper and lower, personal and social factors. The structural principle that man had thus lent to the world from his own, could easily be taken back again when this proved to be necessary for re-constructing the relationship between man and the world.

The significance of such procedure becomes immediately intelligible in the dramatic reversal of signs and values that took place between Hegel and Feuerbach-Marx. Here a system of the world in which the spiritual and universal was exaggerated so as to absorb completely the free human individual, is transformed into a system of materialistic development of nature and history which pretends to arrive at the free individual—a dialectic which Hegel by no means foresaw. And yet this could not have happened, if Hegel's system had not also been capable of being interpreted anthropologically. The same holds good for the whole trans-formation that comes to pass by a slow and subtle change. The meaning of this development becomes clear as soon as the attempt to insert the new empiricism and mathematical physics into the old view of the world—Nicholas of Cusa and the Florentines—produces the parallel phenomenon of "humanism", whose complicated origins cannot here be traced in detail. Humanism has usually been misinterpreted as a movement of transition from the Christian world of the Middle Ages towards a free personal individualism and the discovery of the world of nature. Yet, historically, it is not essentially related to this contrast, but is primarily a stage in the shifting of the centre of the world towards man. To see this, we need only consider the works of a Leonardo, a Dürer or a Michelangelo. To read anti-Christian tendencies into them would be unjust; but we must acknowledge that in their work the microcosm, man, is becoming the centre and measure of nature. It is true that in their paintings and descriptions a natural environment appears for the first time; but it is there only for the sake of man. The anatomy of man, such as it is executed by Signorelli, Pollaiuolo and the artists named above, cannot be represented on a gold background; it needs nature as its foil. This relationship remains the same for Titian and for Rubens and Rembrandt. It is no accident that Petrarch should have discovered the vastness of nature precisely when reading the tenth book of St Augustine's *Confessions*, where he describes the depth of memory and the immanence of the world in it. In the next century humanistic interests were developed further (Erasmus), and the prodigious genius of Shakespeare showed his Protean possibilities between the extremes of heaven and hell. Psychology and characterology were discovered in his wake; the doctrine of the temperaments and the corresponding attitudes of man towards the world began to attract attention. Every new mood is the origin of a new *Weltanschauung* and thus of a new philosophy. This line of development runs from the Enlightenment to the physiognomy of Lavater and Hamann, to the fragments of Friedrich Schlegel and Hegel's phenomenology, ending in the modern philosophical typologies based on an anthropological foundation.

But the full significance of man appears only where nature in all its parts and at every level is seen to lead up to him. As this convergence becomes more evident, so, too, does its vast extension in time. Instead of six thousand years of world history we are finally faced with half a million years of human history and milliards of years of world history. The natural pre-history of man, too, becomes ever more differentiated, clearly demonstrating of how many various factors his final unity is composed, and how precious and truly unique it is consequently bound to be. Yet this view of nature which establishes it finally as the precondition and basis of man as spirit would have been impossible without the human spirit's transcendence of nature that characterizes the scientific and technical attitude. This audacity of the spirit called forth nature's obedient answer which justified and empowered his Promethean courage. Hence the cosmic whole which he now mastered in principle could no longer be the object of the enthusiastic veneration of a quasi-religious attitude. A region of being that obeys us cannot be above us, it cannot be our God. We may not even lovingly surrender ourselves to it, for the power of command entails a duty both to ourselves as spirit and to nature as our foundation and source. Man has needed centuries of development to understand this and to change his attitude accordingly; though it is a short span if compared with the eons which he spent sheltered in the all of nature as a part and spark of it, being at best its image, unable to conceive anything higher than to reproduce the divine order of the cosmos in the small circle of his private and social household. Again and again man was to take up his old, well-tried plan of the world in order to find his bearings; while his house was collapsing around him, he felt obliged to alter its structure and to produce a synthesis between the traditional past and the future. For the old view had not only been a scientific working hypothesis, it was a view of the world which had deeply affected not only man's idea of himself and of the cosmos, but also the relation of both to God. Far more than merely a physical system is changed when the earth is no longer thought to be stationary, surrounded by spheres of planets which, with their qualitative graduations, reach up to the throne of the Godhead, but when a still more marvellous order is discovered which, however, is merely quantitative, and at first thought to extend to infinity. Since the earth was no longer in the middle between a higher and a lower sphere, man ceased to be the centre of the world in the old sense: having below him stones, plants and animals, and above him the purely spiritual world of the angels with their nine choirs, a world to which he is joined as its lowest member, the least of the spirits, because bound to matter. He was, in fact, merely a questionable device to which, according to the old teaching, God condescended in order to fill the gap left in the spirit-world by the fall of the angels.

These spiritual orders, deprived of their cosmic substratum, now lose their importance for the religious and philosophical consciousness; their place is taken by the sun which becomes the new centre of rest, the natural source of all life and culture. Thus it seemed easiest to hide one's tremors before the quantitative infinities of the universe in a new mystic-cosmological stoicism. From early times this system had had the advantage that by it the cosmic reality could be interpreted both physically and spiritually, hence, even in the new situation, both scientifically and religiously, or, more pointedly still, man could be envisaged as both ruler and subordinate. Leibniz and Spinoza sketched the world view of such a stoic-monistic parallelism, whereas Descartes had at first achieved only a dualism between spirit and extension, which led to an impasse and satisfied no one. The Germans attached themselves particularly to "Saint Spinoza"; he became the Church-Father of Herder and Goethe, though also of Novalis, Friedrich Schlegel and Schelling. Goethe was able to practise scientific research under his auspices without having to give up his antique, almost religious, veneration for nature, hence his obstinate opposition to a wholly dominating science in the *Farbenlehre* and elsewhere. Under his guidance, Novalis and the young Schlegel could assert the unity of mathematics and mysticism, of calcula-tion and adoration, of magicians and saints. Thus they propagated the equality of both the old and the new views of the world in paradoxes that reach in Schlegel an intentional cynicism, in Novalis the ultimate existential acrobatics of thought.

In Schelling all this becomes more mature. Stoic parallelism survives in his teaching on the identity of the real with the ideal, whereas the results of exact science are integrated into a "total" nature that, on account of this identity, is still essentially seen as hierarchical and anthropomorphic. Thus for the time being everything can remain almost unchanged; the cosmic religion with the "sacred star" at its centre haunts Goethe's and Mozart's freemasonry in the *West-Eastern Divan* and *The Magic Flute*, and is always capable of being translated into the Christian language: as once at the time of the *Summa contra Gentiles*, so now with Görres and the ageing Schlegel. Yet the new develop-ment outstrips the attempts to restore the old harmony. Their ineffectiveness can be seen from the constant and increasing fear of a wholly different, materialistic and mechanistic, interpretation of nature, which harasses the belated nature enthusiasts like a nightmare. This ghost from Voltaire, Lamettrie and Helvetius haunts the sensitivity of Jean Paul ("Speech of the dead Christ from the universe that there is no God", the demonic figures in his *Titan*, etc.), it costs Kleist and Wozzek their lives and shakes Balzac to the roots. The materialistic evolutionism dominant in the latter part of the nineteenth century has upset the Stoic balance in favour of the psychical factor, yet it does not for this reason sacrifice the quasi- (and increasingly pseudo-) religious attitude towards the cosmos, as in the case of Nietzsche, Haeckel, Bölsche, Titius and Maeterlinck. Nature's ascendancy over man is still replete with the old spirit of cosmological religious feeling which now (in the *Monistenbund*), completely misinterpreting the actual situation, poses as the modern anti-Christian religion, while a whole crowd of cosmic thinkers (Schuler, Klages, Mombert, Däubler, partly also Derleth) are let loose finally to carry the body of the great Pan to its grave. Today this dance of death has itself perished, for its programme was no longer a serious effort at reconciliation, as in German Idealism, but a mere literary exersise. Natural and technical science are again the order of the day.

The nineteenth century saw a more and more desperate defence of bourgeois romanticism against the progressive technicization of the earth, by which it was steadily supplanted. The romantic magic scenery of castles and hermitages, gnomes and southern *fatamorganas* was abandoned by the very people who invented it. In his *Ahnung und Gegenwart*, Eichendorff sets fire to his own stage furniture. It was indeed high time, for men were already building railway stations, and Marx was working on *Das Kapital*. The poets ran away from technical science: Lenau fled to the Niagara—and what would he say if he saw it today! —Sealsfield to the Red Indians and Aztecs, Platen to the southern coasts of Europe and Freiligrath to Africa. Yet these flights were of no avail through the achievements of Alexander von Humboldt and the great English explorers. In the face of their reasoned and naturalistic attitude, the last desires for cosmic intoxication dissolved and finally abandoned their pristine heights for the lower regions of the adventure stories of Cooper and Karl May, Jules Verne and Bonsels. Yet every now and again there appeared sporadically some remnant of a convincing myth, where the old nature retains its integrity and power over man: in Hermann Melville's *Moby Dick* it is the unforgettable myth of the ocean—yet already whales have now almost ceased to exist. In Saint-Exupéry it is the myth of the pure ether beyond all earthly narrowness and of the pure desert of Africa where his aeroplanes crash. Yet even this romantic of science is pursued by the technical achievement that is about to overtake him: the desert is now crossed by roads and is full of petrol tanks; the South Courier has become safe and unheroic. From Zola's industrial world emerges the untamed monster of blood and instinct teeming with the forces of the earth—but soon Freud will begin to domesticate it.

Nature is no longer an alibi for man, for it leads him patiently and irrevocably back to himself. Modern science has indeed laid hands on hitherto uncultivated nature; even if it still saves and concedes here and there a piece of wild nature, a "national preserve", this, too, depends on its good pleasure and is part of its rational planning. But over and above this, it has understood the whole development of the species as tending towards man, though it is too sober to allow the dreams of Nietzsche, who imagined that, just as hitherto each being produced a new one above itself, so man as a link in the chain of nature would produce the superman. Man is the goal of the upward movement, he sees nature coming towards himself. Thus he is far more intimately related to it than was possible according to the old, literal interpretation of the metaphorical account of Genesis. His "body" is from below; inasmuch as he is "nature", he is the result and the quintessence of all this becoming which he bears in himself; indeed, in Edgar Dacqué's view of evolution, he was from the beginning the compelling entelechy of the whole. He is the goal towards which tends the upward stem of nature; whereas the branches spreading out on the sides retain and make visible the various stages of the species that have failed to develop further. Thus the natural depth of human existence is far more profound than earlier psychology and anthropology had imagined; and Freud and Jung cannot be blamed if they walk also as scientists in the "mysterious way that leads to the interior", though in the wake of their greater predecessors of the time of idealism and romanticism. They are the pioneers of those dimensions of becoming in the field of psychology which the biology of evolution describes from the somatic angle. It is just this that narrows their field. They investigate what is of nature in man, that is to say the preliminary basis and material of his mind. They would (like their brethren, the monistic biologists) be guilty of inverting the whole process, if they were now to mistake the direction of the development they themselves have shown, and to attempt to explain spirit from nature, by making it transcend and lose itself in the latter. This would be contrary not only to the meaning of the upward direction, but also to the attempt by the analysts to mechanize even the natural roots of personal life; the question whether they are prompted by a right intention and a right ideal of man may be left open.

Now all this does not necessarily mean that we should wholly sacrifice the reverent attitude that listens to the language and revelation of nature, such as Goethe and his time had still known it, and instead coldly rationalize and mechanize the whole of inorganic and organic nature, including the natural element in man. Certainly in the first rush of victory science did indeed try to apply to every sphere of life its own simplest and seemingly safest method, that is the principles of mathematics, physics and chemistry. Yet this procedure contradicted its own programme because it was not objective and failed to take into account the special claims of the object. Today this is being recognized, at least in the Western world. It was the principal result of the phenomenological movement to clarify these methodical questions of science and scholarship and to demand for each sphere of knowledge its own appropriate method. The deeper layers of nature will not answer to a superficial questioning, one that is suitable only for the lowest sphere of matter. They need to be viewed in relation to life, as Driesch, Uexküll and Portmann attempted to do; they also admit physiognomic examinations, once practised by the baroque and idealistic characterology and capable of being continued today under the influence, perhaps, of Rudolf Kassner or Max Picard, partly also of Guardini. In this way, the essential achievement of the time of Goethe might be saved, as is proved by the example of Hamann. He was in advance of his time in that he knew how to combine a profound art of reading the hieroglyphs of nature and a prophetic "No" to its rationalistic profanation with a holy sobriety of spirit that would not tolerate an orgiastic abuse of its sacred mysteries. He was able to do this, because he understood nature essentially in the context of *man*, and revered it for his sake, because it communicates God's mysterious words to him. Without succumbing to the pantheistic lusts of later generations, Hamann anticipated what Schelling attempted in the philosophy of his later years, namely to interpret all myth as a basis, a preliminary stage and a material of the divine revelation. If nature is understood as what it is meant to be for man, it can and must speak to us with the language God has given it. The question, however, is whether we do not prevent it from doing so. This will be discussed later.

In the transition from cosmology to anthropology, the myth, being the symbolic language of nature, became the archetype, whether this be understood of primeval history, as by Frobenius and Dacqué, or of the present, as by Jung; for it is quite possible for phylogenesis and ontogenesis to converge, at least in the sphere of the history of mankind. Nevertheless, man has to confront these nature-images of himself as spirit. The soul is not everything, nor is history. However rich the developments of human nature which both dimensions reserve to the human mind, this does not absolve him from judging critically the way in which he has advanced towards himself. He cannot afford to withdraw into a Spenglerian *Kulturmorphologie*, nor may he toss in a sea of libido with its changing breakwaters and patterns. In fact, no "philosophy of life" that is too obviously connected with the declining cosmological epoch may be admitted. Indeed, man is called upon to judge his own history, its value or worthlessness, by the very fact that he now stands where he does—certainly not with an elated feeling of attainment, but with a conviction that his new relation to nature has increased his own responsibility for the decisions of mankind. He cannot shirk his duty to judge, on the grounds that obviously his judgment cannot be absolute. On the contrary, this duty is all the more compelling, because the aspects of which he has become aware are so manifold and are relatively complete.

Hence man's present position in the cosmos can be provisionally defined by the fact that, in whatever mirror of nature he may look, he will always ultimately see himself. He thus resembles Narcissus, even though he may perhaps neither love nor seek his own image, nor be intoxicated by it. The idealists experienced this destiny of meeting oneself for the first time. For Fichte it was abysmal and titanic till, in his last period, the tragic aspect was softened to a mystical self-surrender. It was blissful and sensuous in Novalis' fairy-tale of *Hyazinth und Rosenblütchen* who, representing spirit and nature, finally sink into each other's arms. But neither the pantheistic nor the erotic interpretation was objective. Modern man meets himself objectively; he examines his features in the mirror with the same matter-of-factness as the surgeon analyses a case. He is to himself neither a god nor a "thou". It is true, he must understand that he is the quintessence of nature, hence obliged to interpret as well as to use creation in view of himself; but he regards this not as a romantic and intoxicating idea, but as a serious, indeed rather frightening, task.

Thus philosophy has become anthropology; not as if there existed no reality apart from man, but rather in the sense that all cosmic reality converges upon man, and that man cannot interpret himself with reference to an all-embracing cosmic being. He is the "absolute" of the world, a serving, not an absolute, monarch of it precisely because the world has been entrusted to his care. This predicament will teach him to pray and to look for God. Just because he has matured into technical man without any other home save his own fragile being, he is predestined to become religious man.

When man left the cover of the cosmos by which he had been protected, his first experience could only be one of "being without shelter" (*Ungeborgenheit*). This word is used in a wholly or partly reproachful sense, as if man had got himself into this perilous situation by his own carelessness, and ought to slip back into the old cover as quickly as possible. Nevertheless, it would be more profitable to emphasize the positive and historically necessary sense of this new situation. In it man has lost two things, one that was right in the past, the other that was wrong. The right element in his history, now past, was that his whole intellectual life was embedded in the course of nature. Consequently, he could guide himself and his whole—even his technical—activity by the Stoic "living in accordance with nature" (*physikôs zên*). The wrong element was the deification of this embracing reality, the pantheistic "God or nature". The loss of both aspects of the past is a gain for the present. Because man is no longer—at least not wholly—sheltered in nature, he now becomes truly the master of creation, as the Genesis account makes him. He is in no way surrendered to it, but administers it in responsible service to his Creator and according to its own tendency.

Though there is much that is questionable in modern civilization, as is indeed inevitable in an age of such revolutionary changes,

in man; he alone can effect meeting, he alone can be the epitome of the world because he is embodied spirit; only *as* this totality of the world is he spirit and open to God. This last brings out immediately the distance from the cosmological epoch, in which man found the model of his own spiritual being in the idea of a "pure spirit" above him. Hence the eminent importance of the doctrine of spirits or angels in Scholasticism. The purity of their being was held to be due to their separation from matter, whereas the union of body and soul in man meant either that the brightness of his spirit was darkened (Platonism), or that his intrinsic spiritual inferiority (*infimus in ordine spirituum*) needed the support of a complementary factor which would in a way compensate his lack of spiritual intuition by sense-knowledge and intellectual abstraction. If it be true that the notional and cosmic schema of German Idealism is primarily anthropological (its principal error is its pantheistic tendency to setting up absolutes) and that this kind of thinking is incapable of understanding spirit otherwise than in its basic relation to nature and body, it is clear that philosophy has come to be centred in man. For in the first place, the incorporeal spirit which Christian thought, for the most part, ascribes to the angelic being, can no longer be made easily intelligible to this way of thinking, for it does not come under the phenomenologically comprehensible part of the world's being, but recedes into the mysteries of the divine world of faith that remain inaccessible. Moreover, even if incorporeal spirit be posited as real, it can no longer claim to be higher than the embodied spirit of man simply because it lacks a body, and thus the other function of the angelic beings, their service of man in the context of revelation, is also brought out more clearly. Man today cannot be construed according to any other models in the world except himself, and this obviously does not prejudge anything about man as the image of God and the reflection of the inner life of the Trinity. The idea of man can be found only in him and from him, inasmuch as he is the embodied spirit within the world that is open and capable of encounter. Because he is this centre, he has none above himself save God; this makes him the king of creation. But because he is king he has to serve, not just partially but with his whole being, and is respon-

sible for a double service, of the world for God and of God for
the world. The service of the world and of God in one elevates
man to the dignity of royal freedom. Consequently, the contemplative ideal which gave rise to our greatest cultural heritage by
which we are still living today can survive the death of monarchy
and aristocracy; and in the period of democracy, remains the goal
of every individual.

1. *Man creates meaning in encounter.* Before Leibniz expressed it,
St Thomas knew that the human mind possesses the key to the
meaning of things, not by the presence in it of innate ideas, but
by directing on things its own intellectual light as the means of
apprehending all being. This light is spiritual, hence, despite its
receptivity for the finite, it is active and spontaneous without restriction. It can thus be capable of spiritual interpretation only because
it is the medium of meaning as such, into which the "objective"
can enter, and, bringing its meaning with it and revealing it, can
attain to its true and objectively intended meaning. This total
and universal *a priori* of meaning is difficult to grasp; but it can be
in some way elucidated if it be approached from its more easily
intelligible preliminary, namely from organic sensibility and
specific sense qualities. Colour is only in the eye, sound is only in
the ear; both sense organs apply this medium so that those things
can develop and find themselves in it which the Creator has
evidently prepared, invented and willed for it. It is irrelevant that
the lower existed in time before the higher, receptive element that
offered it space. Even the formal conception of applying and
spreading a medium introduces us into a sphere beyond realism
and idealism, before ascending to the distinctively intellectual and
spiritual. For things are not what they are and are meant to be
—in this case coloured and sounding—outside the sense organ, as
if this were a mere photographic plate passively reflecting what is
already wholly there "outside"; nor is the form of the things
simply subjective, put on the formless and unknowable material
of a "thing in itself" as a means of bringing it into orderly categories; but they find their own objective essence in the medium
of their mutually open subjectivities. If, at the level of sense
experience, this offering of space (*Raumbieten*) is still purely natural

and necessary, at the level of the human mind it is supported and characterized by a person in a way which is at the same time inescapably rational and voluntary; the space of meaning thus opened is a personal space. That is why knowledge that occurs in this space cannot be interpreted by any defective case but solely by the highest, adequate and fully valid one, that is by the meeting of another person. For this is not a special case of knowledge beside others, but that which gives direction to all other cases of intellectual or sense knowledge which are below it, because they are inferior in depth of meaning; they all are, at least inchoatively, forms of meeting and letting meet, and thus of the being-for-another of the world's creatures.

A theory of knowledge that resolutely starts from the case that sets the norm of all knowledge, i.e. the meeting between persons, saves itself a good many false problems. These appear necessarily where the higher is approached from the lower, where the meeting person is ranged among the "objects as such" or "things" and thus can never appear in his own right. However, we do not here mention this true centre of the theory of knowledge in order to develop a detailed personalism, but to elucidate every case from the highest standpoint. In order to fulfil the conditions of objective knowledge, every personal meeting demands an unrestricted openness of one's own person, on principle; this means an advancing of meaning that is not conditioned (*eine nicht-nur-bedingte Vorstreckung von Sinn*), concretely a preparedness to admit another and let him assert himself, to love objectively and unselfishly; and this form of personal openness cannot be missing from any other form of knowledge. In other words: there is no "purely theoretical" attitude of knowledge that would not be at least in its root also a wholly human and true (*gesamtwahrheitlich*) attitude. Man as a whole performs his act and is responsible for it; indeed, in his intellectual and spiritual acts he is always present as a whole and appears in them in his indivisible essence. To all things and beings that appear in the cosmos he opens himself as that wherein meaning can be found; offering himself as a medium where, in the light of the human spirit, he certainly proves himself as that which is in principle capable of all truth and of being changed into all things and conditions (*anima quodammodo omnia*). But he is so not primarily in order to dominate, but to render a service constantly renewed by a human existence fully understood and affirmed.

To an epoch in which anthropology has been recognized as the key to philosophy, it is self-contradictory to foster an intelligence that approaches things from a merely rationalistic and technical point of view, indeed it completely misunderstands its own being. This is the point of the warnings sounded by all those contemporaries who understand the situation, however different their views may otherwise be: by Scheler or Heidegger or Jaspers, by Bernanos or Buber or Aldous Huxley. No technical achievements can dispense us from the necessity of gaining this insight; even though things may ever more rapidly jump through all the hoops we extend to them, may ride all bicycles, and by their readiness to obey, hypnotize, rather than be hypnotized by, their trainer. Admittedly, man's success with things is due to man, to the right use of his reason that is *a priori* in relation to them; yet he should never forget that his reason is always the reason of a man, of one who wholly offers and gives himself because he cannot do otherwise, because in this freely accepted duty he is burdened with the responsibility for the destiny of the world. In the meeting between man and things the latter answer in proportion as man opens and surrenders himself; there is no other, less exacting way of creating truth, today less than ever. In the cosmological period a certain naïve realism and objectivism was still adequate, inasmuch as the measure of truth was primarily situated in the embracing cosmic order. In the anthropological period the highest objectivity can be attained only by the highest personal risk of man himself; for he cannot attain to what he is, that is the free and understanding spirit above nature, in any other way save by the ever renewed use of his freedom by which he, far from being made in advance, is always newly designed and realized. It is indeed consoling that this freedom that risks itself has a highest and freest master above and within itself, whose providence directs even the risk; but this does not for a moment absolve man from taking it. For God's providence is not a "natural order", nor a Hegelian "world spirit" to which the human spirit could simply entrust itself, expecting to be conveyed by this higher reason to the invisible goal. In the game of the world the stake is no less than man himself.

The practical consequences of this affect every sphere of knowledge. Detailed work on individual departments and their immanent laws (such as Dilthey, Spranger and Nicolai Hartmann have undertaken) may indeed be valuable, yet human life cannot be so confined; in whatever sphere the individual be engaged, he must always act in his entirety. The dignity of the scholarly and scientific attitude demands that every scientific judgment should be pronounced with the universal idea of man in view, and, consequently, as coming from, and pointing towards, man. It must come from the man who is given the responsibility for this judgment; he can never escape it by imagining that in this case he is called in merely as a theoretician, an aesthetic expert or a sociologist; he is asked always as the indivisible, freely responsible person that he is. It must point towards man, whom he will then invariably consider in his judgments and actions. This does not only envisage the practical point of view, as being concerned with the possible consequences of a truth, with inventions and their application, social measures and so forth. It is also important theoretically, in the way an individual judgment fits into the total truth about man. Thus we may prove the result of a piece of research to be misleading merely by applying it to the human context, even though in isolation it cannot be impugned. For example, the well-known American statistics on the sexual behaviour of man and woman is conspicuously divorced from any anthropological framework: the *sexual* behaviour of men is always a *human* sexual behaviour, and thus has a meaning and importance which the expert must have explicitly and constantly in view if he is not to miss the mark. This holds good also if the "object", in this case American man, probes himself no more deeply than his questioner. If he had been questioned more deeply and adequately, the investigation would perhaps have yielded more correct and objective results than the "object" could have produced if left to himself.

To give another example: take the examination of a great work of art belonging to the past, say a poetic work of Goethe or Schiller. It is evident that the person who examines it must possess the necessary aesthetic equipment, both objective, scientific knowledge and subjective, delicate sensitiveness for aesthetic values, and that the examination has to start from these. Yet it is certain that the poet did not mean to create a work that was to be confined to the world of aesthetic values, but that he wanted to express his own humanity in the language of art, and, even more, to touch other men by putting before them the highest and most exacting ideal of man. Hence, even in the perspective of the poet, the aesthetic aspect is transcended by the integrally human. On the other hand, the interpreter cannot be satisfied with understanding and evaluating this transcendence in its historical setting. He has to communicate with the poet in the universal idea of man which is the intellectual sphere common to them both, and to deliver his own aesthetic judgment in function of this conception of which, in the final analysis, even aesthetic values depend. Thus it is in no way a violation of the functions of a critic for Guardini to question whether Rilke can really take full responsibility as a man for what he says about life and man in his *Duinese Elegies*, which, as he says himself, are meant to be philosophical and religious statements. The same applies to Reinhold Schneider, who asks the same question of the great creators of culture of German Idealism, for example of Schiller with regard to his *Wallenstein*, or of Kleist, Brentano and others. This is no dreary application of moral standards to aesthetic values; but it does mean that the latter are anchored in a deeper and more comprehensive sphere which the aesthetic world must reflect, if it would not be irresponsibly degraded to some kind of beautiful make-believe and thus unwillingly would bear witness to a negation of philosophy.

This does not mean that the critic of the great works of the past should judge them by the standards of the present or even of his own limited subjectivity. On the contrary, we are concerned with an ever fresh encounter on the personal plane; the more deeply the enquirer questions, the richer is the meaning he elucidates; further, the more profound the man or the work of the past are in themselves, the more significant and intimate will be the communication. The enquirer will first humbly and willingly receive whatever can be learned from the object itself, even the categories according to which it must be considered, in order to be instructed by the object itself before himself pronouncing a judgment. Nevertheless, breadth of mind does not mean refusal to take up a definite attitude, and liberality is not a shirking of responsibility.

In medieval philosophy, the categories of encounter existed only in rudimentary form, because the "thou" remained subsumed under the abstract notion of the object. Even in Idealism they were not developed, because this was concerned with a perpetual encounter of the abstract ego or of the objective and absolute spirit with itself. In principle the equation of anthropology and philosophy is reached with Kant; in his posthumous handbook of logic the content of philosophy is characterized by the fourth, concluding question: "What is man?" Feuerbach's anti-Hegelian manifesto (*Principles of the Philosophy of the Future*, 1843) declares point-blank: "Modern philosophy makes man the sole and universal object of philosophy, that is it makes anthropology the universal science." Marx and Nietzsche agreed with him; nevertheless, it is only in the twentieth century that this "man" is no longer seen as a materialistic or evolutionary phantom, but as the concrete human being, the individual person within the community. Martin Buber has described the advent of dialogic thought in his postscript to the *Dialogic Writings* (1953) and in his *Problem of Man* (1947). As a representative of the dialogical religion he was predestined to further this idea. According to his universalistic conception of Judaism, this religion is explicitly and obviously what man as such represents in a hidden and fragmentary way. This view allows him to find parallels in the most varied Christian thinkers, in the works of Ebner and Mounier, Gabriel Marcel, Emil and August Brunner, of Scheler and Jaspers. In Catholic circles, the practical wisdom of Peter Lippert gained the idea ready admittance, in that he made the encounter with the personal God in the human "thou" of Jesus Christ the primary case of knowledge at its simplest. In the second volume of his *Philosophy*, Jaspers intensified considerably the idea of communication. What for Kant was still outside the sphere of philosophy, now became the starting point of every serious theory of knowledge, namely an object that cannot be constituted by the categories of the knowing subject, and precisely as such must be the knowable that is to be known (not a "thing in itself"), in other words, the human person in his freedom and responsibility. The freedom of the other must be admitted, and this implies the impossibility of anticipating its decisions and self-revelation. But this can happen only where one's own reason is more than an isolated capacity of knowing, but is rooted in an equally free and responsible totality of the person.

However, this is not enough. The encounter of such an alien freedom within the sphere of one's own personal freedom cannot be suffered to take place as between two sovereign and absolute quantities, either of which could be aware of the other's sovereignty by reason of its own (in the way a ruler receives another of equal rank in his own territory with the same honours he knows to be due to himself). Such a "pluralism" of subjects would only be a relapse into a solipsistic theory of knowledge that built up everything alien from logical conclusions or psychological analogies of one's own enclosed and self-contained ego. The very capacity of letting a "thou" appear in its uniqueness and personal dignity, can be situated only in that region of the ego where, transcending itself, it is responsible to an absolute "Thou". If it were otherwise, the ego would always take its own intellectual light as the standard by which to measure the thou, and precisely for this reason this "thou" could never appear before and in him in his free, independent being. The personal knowledge of a co-ordinated "thou" can take place only in the sphere where both created persons know themselves responsible before the eternal "Thou" and meet each other before the veiled throne of the eternal judge. Every spiritual person receives his highest dignity and freedom from his relation to God; for a person cannot be viewed and recognized in any other way. For as knowable, the person is himself only where he is freely responsible before the Eternal One, and he can be recognized by the ego only because this, as knowing, is open in principle before the absolute "Thou" (*cogito, ergo sum*). The knowing ego has not two windows, one towards God and one towards man; but because God looks into its window (and only thus is a window constituted) it can look out of the window towards a human "thou", and through this on to other beings and objects in the world.

Inter-subjectivity is the crux of all philosophy. It is, however, ruled out from the beginning if a philosophy starts with an abstract ego that has to manoeuvre itself out of its prison by syllogisms, or with a total ego in the idealistic sense, of which the individual consciousness would be but an "empirical" limitation. We are far from identifying God with inter-subjectivity, let alone with the absolute ego of the Idealist; nevertheless, we must admit that a true encounter can take place only in God and in his sight. This means it can happen only where created persons share in God's uniqueness and freedom, because they are open to God and hence, in principle, also to each other, without the one being entitled to call the other to judgment before the tribunal of his own knowledge and freedom. A theory of knowledge dealing with the meeting between human beings can only be established on a religious basis. This is the price that has to be paid if man is no longer regarded (cosmologically) as one "nature" among other natures, that is in the abstract as one "subject of knowledge" among other such subjects that are to be treated in an equally abstract way. It is true, his openness to the world makes him the creator of meaning (*Sinnstifter*) for the latter, and this not only in the sense still prevalent in the Middle Ages, as one whose abstract capacity enables him to read and elicit ready-made meanings that God has placed in things. Yet he cannot create these meanings autonomously, as if he were an absolute spirit, but only as one responsible to God to the very roots of his whole person, one ready to serve and listen. He is given the task to rule creation in precisely the measure as he fulfils this ideal. In exactly the measure as he listens to God, he can speak to the world an essential word on behalf of God, and he can also really hear his neighbour and, listening, can see him (*loquere ut videam te*—"speak so that I may see thee"). And beginning to see what the other is and ought to be before God, he can become a neighbour to him, giving help and creating meaning. In this alone consists under-standing. The knowledge of partial truths, of individual spheres of creation and of the history of the world and mankind, as well as the investigation of the material world in its usefulness for man, in short, whatever wants to share in the act of understanding, it all remains enclosed in that all-embracing form of it which gives all knowledge its meaning. It may be somewhat humiliating for the history of the spirit that this elementary law should have needed thousands of years to dawn on us. It is nevertheless consoling that the *kairos* of this understanding is just this present time, which, in other respects, is decried as wickedly materialistic and utilitarian, and which indeed decries itself as such. But making the real living human being the centre of philosophy will have its consequences. It is simply a law of man's life that he must look for his God and for his neighbour, and in doing so can neither behave as an absolute ego nor as an abstract subject, but only as an ego conversing with its thou by question and answer. And this law will make itself heard above all the noise of machines. Here, too, lies the ultimate solution of the struggle between the warring ideologies of the Eastern and the Western worlds, which, from the point of view of the philosophy of history, are already reconciled in principle.

2. *Man as corporeal is in solidarity with the cosmos.* Meeting, viewed "from the higher to the lower", takes place through spatiality. It does this in a twofold sense. On the one hand, thought is definitely convinced of the objectivity of the non-ego by the violence of the shock when bodies impinge on each other, exclude each other in space, and fight for a place in the sun. On the other hand, man as a corporeal being recapitulates the stages of the cosmos in himself, feeling and experiencing the world as a whole. Moreover, in virtue of his being a spirit in a body, he not only contains in himself both plant and animal, but is able to understand them in their inner origin even under the formal dimensions of space and time. Now it is true that man has always experienced the brutality of a body that hit him; but formerly it was possible to him by means of idealism and "interiorization" (*Verinnerlichung*) to withdraw from the sphere where he was abandoned to crude and tragic accidents. Chinese, Indians and Greeks vied with each other in conquering the necessity of bodily suffering. Thus the second aspect did, indeed, already exist, since idealist thinkers have always attempted to deduce sensuality *a priori*, either as a fall of the spirit from which it must save itself,

or as a condition of the spirit through which it can find itself. What is new in the present situation is that modern man can no longer use the idealistic escape when meeting the "thou": he must stand up to the shock. Nor can he be satisfied with an *a priori* deduction from above, from the spirit: he must see himself as a being of nature, becoming by rising from below, through all the stages by which the concrete cosmos develops. He can see himself no longer as a "guest" or "stranger" in the world, who has come down from above, as the Christian followers of the Platonists still like to see man. He comes from below not only in his purely material being, as the scriptural image of the slime of the earth might be superficially interpreted. Plants and animals in their variety are not only slime, but life, indeed ascending life directed in its meaning towards man. This fact of having developed out of preliminary stages struck the men of the nineteenth century so forcibly that at first they saw nothing else. It needed a new effort to harmonize the aspect of evolution with that of the qualitative difference between spirit and nature. Perhaps this last, boldest leap from sub-spiritual nature to man was but the last of those mysterious leaps, mutations and macro-evolutions in the ascending line of being. Might it not be possible that between the evolutionary periods the too tight skin or cocoon bursts to bring to light the new creature that has been formed within? "The entelechy, man, is the metaphysical meaning permeating the whole tree of life; hence 'man', as the last and highest being, is the 'primal form' (*Urform*) of the whole organic world, just as he is from the standpoint of evolution, whereas all physical formation . . . is the unfolding of the inner primal form of man." Hence one would have to

draw a genealogical tree on which all real, present or primeval, living beings are side branches, none of which leads to man immediately; in other words, the required central trunk of the tree of life fails to exist in the physical animal forms of natural history, but so far exists only ideally. Now, if organic nature is interiorly a unity, as we have good reason to assume, and if all development ultimately leads to man, then the entelechy, "man", is precisely this central trunk connecting all the rest; it is the ever-present, potential primal form, because the whole genealogical tree is that of man, to whom all real natural beings are directed like so many side branches.[1]

If this is true—and everything does, indeed, point to such a universal connexion—then there is, indeed, in man a synthesis of nature and spirit, these terms being taken in the sense of Idealism. For the spiritual nature of man can be determined neither solely from below (as a quantitative elevation, in the manner of Darwinism), nor solely from above (as understood by Fichte and Hegel)—nature as that which spirit proposes for itself, in order to become conscious of itself. But this "synthesis" can no longer be understood in the dualistic sense of current philosophy, namely as the conjunction of two opposed metaphysical elements: cosmological *eros* and transcendent spirit (so Klages); a surge from below, and a spiritual, but ineffective, recognition of values from above (as Scheler formulates it in connexion with Schopenhauer's categories of the blind will and the impotent concept). This fashionable dualism certainly reflects the contemporary experience that the mind (as a separate intellectual function in the sense of the Enlightenment) is incapable of mastering reality as a whole. But this desperate experience that the mastery of nature cannot be understood so cheaply, however disillusioning for modern man, suggests at the same time that a period of deeper self-interpretation is about to dawn for him. He is the epitome of the cosmos, the *Weltidee* (Dempf), and, as such, a master and king of the whole, risen from below. He is the head of nature, which, however, no longer appears merely as a kingdom subject to him, but as his natural "mystical body". He cannot be divorced from this body, not even for the sake of God. This necessitates a new form of asceticism, which will be found less in a spiritualistic turning away from the world, but rather in a mastery of nature due to the mind as king—but much asceticism is demanded from a king! We have already pointed out that, on the one hand, in this onto- and phylo-genetic proximity to man, nature is even more than before the immense sounding board of the spirit, such as the romantics saw it. On the other hand, being unmistakably directed to the evolution of man, it does not exist to inebriate the spirit, but to be as a garden and orchard, in which the spirit always remains the

[1]Edgar Dacqué, *Natur und Erlösung*, 1933; pp. 129-131.

master. Thus the relation between man and nature remains dialectical: he is its dreaded master who disposes of it according to his good pleasure: "And let the fear and dread of you be upon all the beasts of the earth, and upon all the fowls of the air, and all that move upon the earth: all the fishes of the sea are delivered into your hands." (Gen. 9. 2.) And yet nature needs to look for this master, to wait "for the revelation of the sons of God . . . in hope that nature will also be delivered from the servitude of corruption, into the liberty of the glory of the children of God." (Rom. 8. 19-21.) This dialectic applies to nature; it is not valid for man who, on the contrary, has ceased to confront nature dialectically, since he is no longer seen as "part", but as the goal and epitome of the cosmos. Now, he is unmistakably allotted the administration of the natural sphere; again, not in arbitrary absolutism, but in the free responsibility that is due to his Creator, and in subjection to the divine Providence that guides both him and the cosmos.

This double freedom (*analogia libertatis*), indeed, is the source of conflicts man must face both now and in the future. By subjecting nature to man's reason, God has admitted him into that interior sphere of laws whose equilibrium, intended by the Creator to support the spiritual and intellectual life of mankind, is self-adjusting, but is bound to be disturbed by man's interference. He can neither sublimate nature into spirit nor change it into a technical mechanism completely at the disposal of his intellect, but must reckon with a mysterious autonomy and proper value of the natural creation as something permanent, whereas his own interference with nature will necessarily be in some way problematic, and the more so the more deeply it penetrates into the harmony of the world. Everything is being subjected to technical methods: the growing processes in nature as well as in man himself; the landscape, to such a degree that it loses its natural and spontaneous character; the economy of the human organism, and even the unconscious spheres of man's soul, whose maternal darkness is lit up by the artificial light of psychoanalysis; the higher powers of the soul, too, by the deliberate practice of suggestion and contemplation. There is no sphere into which the process of rationalization has not penetrated; in fact, it goes so

far as to aim at an artificial unconsciousness, an artificial spontaneity and naïvety, a "synthetic childhood" (Novalis) as the
highest products of the spirit. Yet the true secret of nature as
"freedom that appears" (Schiller) and spontaneous grace as it
becomes visible in the beauty of childhood and youth, points
immediately to the Creator and, by definition, cannot be produced of set purpose.

The ideal of the marionette is the death of all living art and
nature. Hence man's "culture", that has imperceptibly passed over
into the "technical age", retains henceforth a deeply questionable,
even tragic aspect, which can be countered only by a new human
ethos, that of man's responsibility to himself and to nature. He
must use technical possibilities discreetly and sparingly, guided by
the ideal of man who, being spirit, cannot be just a purely
evolutionary product of nature in the Marxian sense. The greatest danger of our time is that large sections of mankind are
guided by false and outdated concepts of man. It may, perhaps
be necessary for peoples in a primitive stage of civilization
and religion to be incited, indeed brutally compelled, to skip
thousands of years of organic development in order to adapt
themselves to the cultural and living standards of our technical
civilization. For surely these Asiatic temples of idols and the
horrible distorted masques from Africa and the South Sea Islands
have no place in our world, though a decadent European art
may extol them as the last word. It may even seem understandable
that Communism (not the Christian missions), giving short shrift
to these outmoded things, should create in such peoples a *tabula
rasa* from which a tolerably fruitful contact between nations and
cultures may become possible. Yet such a process is fraught with
great danger; for it means not only "educating" savages, but
also preparing highly developed civilizations for a degenerate
materialistic and nihilistic form of Western thought, which
expresses the resentments of the inventors of this secularized
Messianism.

Christianity will have to make contact with a *Weltanschauung*
which, even at its highest, no longer aspires to the Absolute
as did the great religions of the past, but is attached to a crude
this-worldly outlook. This dark, rude brother to which it

will henceforth be chained is not sentimental, it is little concerned with the well-being of the subhuman cosmos. He sees in that only "material" useful to man. But the body has another function. It reminds us of the crude concreteness of things and especially of our fellow-men: their mere existence, their needs, also their stupidity—so many things that, as Christians, we are perhaps often prepared to "bear" only from a distance and in theory, and of which the romantic philosopher of nature and the body never thought at all. All this, which we find sufficiently unbearable if it hits us in the eye, will probably become highly topical. As "technicians" we are so anxious to free this bodily sphere from its demonic depths, to cure it, to fit it with drainage and disinfect it. We indulge in private and public physical culture; in fact sport has become the religion of the masses, though no longer, as in ancient Greece, balanced by the intellectual and religious interest of the nation, but as one immense business enterprise and as the gigantic temple of the body that is deifying itself. We have sterilized hospitals and operating theatres, psychiatric sessions and other institutions designed to work systematically on the human material. We are indeed almost exclusively occupied with this corporeal sphere, since we approach and solve even intellectual and spiritual matters almost entirely as statistic and organic problems. Yet this sphere will not fail to clutch at us with the whole faceless and abysmal, indeed Asiatic, demonry of lower nature; and as yet it is by no means decided who will be the victor in this uncanny duel. Only one thing is certain: we cannot escape by flight from the enterprise we have begun, but must, also as Christians, penetrate the corporeal sphere even more effectively by the spirit. Even though every young man and woman must take up the same personal struggle, in principle a certain magic charm of the material depth has been broken. The body and its secrets, once so prudishly hidden and hence alluring, are today only too openly exposed, whether on the couch of the surgeon, of the analyst or of the statistician of sexual behaviour. What is most needed is to give back to this poor, humiliated piece of humanity a spiritual home, a small sphere of innocent life. Casuistry will be of little use; the questionable materialistic cures will again have to be themselves healed by a new ethos, sprung from the centre of Christianity which, after all, is the religion of the Incarnation, of en-fleshing.

We have spoken above of the ethos of "encounter" and the responsibility for total (*gesamtheitliche*) truth which this places on man. Thence evolves on him a new responsibility for the forms of bodily representation of himself in all spheres of the cosmos. From early times rulers have been concerned to erect monuments of their creative power in history, such as pyramids and triumphal arches. But today as never before we are all involved in impressing the human countenance on nature, and we are all responsible for the face it will finally receive: it may be that of a wall, besmirched and scribbled on by stupid and vicious hands, or that of a painting hard to interpret but generously conceived. Things are made even more difficult by the fact that we have to speak in the plural. The time of the Pharaohs and of the Roman and Christian emperors and kings is past, when one man, representing the many, could impress his personal form on the whole. When the end of this age was in sight only two ways seemed still to be open: either one could follow Hegel and Marx, in whose philosophy a more or less impersonal and objective world spirit takes its necessary course regardless of the individual; or one could be one of the tragic individuals who, fighting the mass and necessarily defeated, could yet once more impress something like a form: form as an exclamation mark, visible only to a few individuals akin to themselves. From Kierkegaard to Ebner, Haecker and the group contributing to *Der Brenner* all that was "spirit" in Christianity was unquestioningly on this side. And it became a sort of silent agreement that the true Church could consist only of individuals, and that God could call man only as an individual. Now it is true that the Church cannot be a mass; but it is equally true that she is a community, and especially so for the individual. Christians are united in a common responsibility as regards the Church, but are also associated with their brethren to build a common, fully embodied human world. We must get used to the concept of collective responsibility which, it is true, can be based on the free consent of persons, yet which is something other than the mere consent of solitary consciences.

"Moral Rearmament" demonstrates to a surprised world the

phenomenon of genuine responsibility borne by individuals who see themselves as members of one another. This phenomenon is situated in Christianity without which it would be unthinkable. But it necessarily transcends the specifically Christian and passes over into the human sphere, appealing from the Christian point of view to the human conscience in every individual, including those outside Christianity, and this gives the movement its power and attraction. It is here mentioned only as a symptom, not for the sake of its concrete effects. But as such it must attract our attention. For this movement establishes the connexion between the necessarily solitary contemplation in which man looks and listens to God, confessing his guilt—which can also only be done personally—and the action that has necessarily also its technical and organized side, uniting both in the community as their centre. It is quite possible that much is conceived too superficially, too much from the moral and too little from the religious point of view, that the movement is too activist, and leaves out of account the depths of suffering, the fruitfulness of failure and defeat; in fact it may be too utilitarian and "American". Yet the basic idea is right. It is difficult to find the balance which must always be sought anew. There is on the one hand a false modesty of the spirit that is secretly ashamed of being in the body and hence will always, in the best Platonic-spiritualist manner, deny its links with the community and its solidarity with all others for better or for worse. On the other hand, there is danger of a complacency of the spirit in communal practices, which may easily degenerate into a mutual spiritual exhibitionism of weaknesses and virtues and thus into a moral Pharisaism. The way is narrow, but we must walk in it. The need is so urgent that it really calls for the saint who would give himself, his everyday existence and his inmost soul for his brethren. Such a man would show no individualistic melancholy of the isolated ego, but would put his hand to the common task, transferring all ascetic practice to the inner sphere of mind and will, in order to gain the impetus necessary for shaping the external world without surrendering to body and matter. All this would have to be done as a task entrusted to man by God, not in the spirit of building a Babylonian tower or an earthly paradise. Such a human idea might hope also to bring light, strength and guidance to the masses. But this anticipates the second part of this treatise, in which we shall deal with the Christian form of this age.

The last point that is to be made at the moment concerns the fearful responsibility of man for the shaping of the world, as a free agent under providence. Man has always had this task, but its magnitude has never struck him with such force as now, when the whole subhuman cosmos begins to stir in response to his call like a giant awakened from sleep. Until now man has always been able to appeal to the power of a nature that embraced him, which smilingly suffers the children of man to play on the beach by the sea and serenely destroys their work, perhaps even integrates their most beautiful achievements into the greater harmony of the spheres. Goethe (*Nature and Art*) still looked at things in this way. That man should ever be in a position to alter the face of nature was inconceivable, even for the poet of *Prometheus* (Goethe) or for Schelling, who wrote on the essence of human freedom (*Das Wesen der menschlichen Freiheit*). But the fact that man can implies that he legitimately may govern nature, and this involves making independent decisions in the spirit of his absent master. The efficient administrator or steward must not have a slave mentality, else he will lack the intellectual stature needed for such decisions. Yet neither may he play the master, else he will no longer be the steward. The figure of the steward plays a memorable rôle in the Gospels. This should teach man in the sphere of creation what is demanded of him when he is allowed to be God's representative in the world. In the entirely novel conditions of the present it needs humility, indeed, so to apply oneself to the mind of God as to find the right way. And it also needs wide vision to apprehend the sublime function of man in the world, and to judge consistently by that standard.

This does not invalidate the laws of matter, of world economy, of production and the world politics resulting from them. To assume this would be starry-eyed idealism. But we may never tolerate the co-existence of more or less cynical realism in action with an idealistic cultural ethics, such as Scheler has recently suggested. As realism becomes universal, transcending parties, nations and continents, it will normally have a unifying effect.

Machiavellism might indeed continue to direct a particular state, but it would only be permanently harmful when mankind has come to regard itself as a single whole. The struggle of individual interests will be integrated into the pursuit of the common interest, and the very fact that this exists will also bring about the reconciliation of the struggle of ideologies which seem virtually already past. It is true, a long and painful period may elapse before history will reach this stage, though it can already be envisaged; but this is irrelevant. The simultaneous opening of the technical and natural-historical spheres has brought about a revolution: man masters nature, from which he himself had arisen as a natural being; but this revolution is still in its infancy, and so the consciousness of mankind has understandably not yet assimilated it, and responds with all sorts of eccentric and pathological reactions. New power and success are at first going to its head; the old intellectual and spiritual equipment proves to be unsuitable when transferred and applied to the new problems. The deeper and mystical layers of tradition give little help to come to grips with the new tasks. They make their own claims but fail to show how these can be integrated into the universal task of man. They are concerned with transcendence in its purest form, but they fail to show how this can harmonize with the immanent tasks of mankind, or, indeed, how it fits into the common responsibility of mankind the more easily, precisely because it is the highest function of spirit. True, we should not know the meaning of transcendence if we were to turn it into a mere medium or motive force for a more complete mastery of immanence. And yet, if we now approach this third factor, it will not be possible to consider it in isolation from the other two, even for a moment. The time of isolationism is past, both for the spirit and for religion, for, through the body, we are bound to the cosmos as a whole. Only in union with it is the human spirit meant to be perfected and to find its shelter in the eternal sphere of the Divine.

3. *Man as spirit is open to God.* The third thesis that describes the situation of modern man in its upward direction sounds at first like a mere repetition of the traditional one that has governed

anthropology and metaphysics from Plato to German Idealism:
spirit is the *locus* of openness to Being itself, outside which there
is mere nothingness. Openness means light, reflexion, awareness
of oneself, not only incipient (animal) but perfected interiority.
Indeed, the spirit itself is this light; it is not only illumined by
it, it does not only receive it as a gift externally from above.
As *intellectus agens* the spirit itself is light, as we must constantly
maintain against the Platonists. Yet it does not enjoy absolute
dominion over this light. It cannot identify itself with it, it
possesses the light only by receiving it. Mind is not receptive
in its sensual sphere while being spontaneous and autonomous
qua spirit; it is receptive also in its intellectual spontaneity.
The tenth Book of the *Confessions* of St Augustine describes
how by degrees the thinker is inescapably overwhelmed by
this insight. Overawed, he first enters into the depths of
his own mind, "into the large halls of the memory, where
are the treasures of the innumerable images which the
senses have gathered from all manner of things". Whatever
belongs to the world, material and spiritual things have their
place in it. But the mind also knows about God, and thus God,
too, seems to have his place in it; and St Augustine assembles the
reasons why the "blessed life" in God is one with the deepest
memory, and the truth of human life is inseparable from absolute
truth. Yet the mind does not recognize eternal truth as its own
light: "Nor yet art thou the mind itself; because thou art the
Lord God of the mind; and all these are changed, whereas thou
remainest unchangeable over all. . . . Where therefore did I find
thee so that I might learn thee, except in thee above myself? . . .
O Truth, thou art everywhere present to all who ask thy advice
and answerest all at the same time, though they ask thy counsel
on various matters. Thou answerest clearly, but not all hear thee
clearly. All consult thee on what they want, but they do not always
hear what they want. He is thy best servant who is not so much
concerned to hear from thee what he himself wants, but rather
to want what he hears of thee." (10, 25f.)

  This theme of St Augustine's will always continue to be heard.
The light of the human mind is a listening, a dialogical, light.
"He was not the light, but was to give testimony of the light."

(John 1. 8.) There is no question of either autonomy or hetero-
nomy; in fact Kant's alternative misses the secret of the mind's
being. But there is in the self, in the *autos*, the greater which,
being the absolute, cannot be described as "another", a *heteron*.
Fichte struggled magnificently with this mystery; having overcome, by the true idea of the absolute ego, Kant's objection that
God's positive law might be "another", he finally penetrated to
the dialogical situation, in which the finite submits to the infinite Spirit, so as to be spirit precisely in this. Hegel, in his young
days, knew about this mystery, as also Schleiermacher. Schelling
came to realize it more and more, Goethe possessed it, Stifter and
Jean Paul lived by it, Novalis and Hölderlin found it in the end:
this act of surrender, of the open "listening" as St Augustine
called it, is the last, redeemed formula of German Idealism,
which is only superficially crossed and dimmed by a pantheistic
ideology. Thence the message sounds also into our philosophy,
which is proved by almost every name, quite apart from the
authentically Christian ones. There are, first, Heidegger and
Jaspers, and, of course, Martin Buber, and Ortega and Croce
(the author of the famous pages "Why we cannot call ourselves
anything but Christians") and Bergson and Huxley and Kassner
and Rilke in his first two Elegies and the *Late Poems*. For the
moment it is comparatively unimportant whether these thinkers
attain to a revelation given from above, or whether they interpret
human reason as a being open to the unknown, the ineffable, a
listening into silence, into the salvation and sanctity of Being as
such, as does Heidegger, consciously basing himself on Hölderlin.
What is important is the fundamental experience that the light of
being is not "at hand" like the immanent, ever burning light of
the active intellect. In order to know it, the mind cannot simply
let shine its own light, illuminating with it the objects of this world,
but needs a "grace". Aristotle and the great Arabs knew that, and
William of Auvergne, though awkwardly, tried to assert it
against the victorious doctrine of scholasticism. This "grace"
implies a revelation as a sign that the spirit is about to cross the
threshold of the profane and enter into the realm where God
makes himself felt—even though only a foretaste of the *possibility*
of his appearance. Now, however, it is seen that we can never

totally separate the ("immanent") light of the mind, its spontaneity, the being-in-act of the active intellect from this highest light, which constitutes precisely the mind's being mind, its transcendence to the world. It is true, too, as those thinkers never cease to tell us, that the mind destroys itself and crumbles if it splits into an inferior and a superior mind, an autonomously functioning reason (*Verstand*) and a *ratio* (*Vernunft*) that is reserved for special philosophical and religious purposes.

This will be seen most easily from what has been said about encounters between human beings. Here we were concerned with a creation (*Stiftung*) of truth that has nothing to do with an idealistic-categorical treatment of matter existing for the senses; it is, on the contrary, a work of personal self-giving, of a trusting self-advance in which the "thou" (or the object as such) can show and unfold itself as it is. Though this "creating" is the actual spontaneity of the human mind involving its sovereignty and freedom, it is nevertheless no arbitrary, subjective action, but something that must be demanded by a highest light, and for which man must take responsibility before this light. The "creator of meaning" (*Sinnstifter*) is under a secret obedience which constitutes his dignity and freedom. Anyone ignorant of this duty of obedience would not have a right to be credited with "mind". Such a person would be one who, deliberately or otherwise, classed the light given to his mind among the *objects* or the *means* of knowledge. Being itself is not an individual being in the creaturely sense, even though that which deserves to be called mind and person shines forth only through its irradiation and inspiration. It is, indeed, true that we can recognize that which is only in the light of Being; and seen in this way, Being is that by which a thing is recognized (*esse, quo cognoscitur res*). Yet this "by which" is not to be summed up in the same way as the other "conditions of the possibility of objective knowledge" are made intelligible as the interior structure of the mind. This may be unpleasant for the scientific intelligence, yet here is its last chance to save and justify itself as an activity worthy of man. The reality on which all hangs is the real relation between man and God. Seen in this light, everything in the world is elevated to the reality of man and shares through him in the radiance which the absolute, eternal truth sheds on the temporal, relative world. In the inviolable encounter with the eternal, genuine meeting will ever and again happen in the world. And this first encounter of man with God does not depend on the good pleasure of man, as if he could be spirit or "mere nature" according to his liking; it rests on the will of God who, creating, has determined to reveal himself to finite beings (whether through creation itself or in a yet higher way) so that man can only choose to be what he is or to deny this, without yet being able to destroy it.

All this, however, does not yet characterize the present situation as one essentially different from the interpretation of the world that has prevailed until now. The difference lies in that the suggested transcendence of intellectual (*geistig*) knowledge (as the intellectual and spiritual aspect of human existence before God) is now probably for the first time seen in its proper peculiarity and no longer seems to fit into the cosmological categories. Now it is true, the ancients, too, knew that the human person cannot be understood as "nature" and "entelechy" in the same sense as the subhuman beings, which provide themselves from their surroundings with the appropriate necessities allotted to them by the Creator, which they do not by freely reasoned decision but by natural instinct. Inasmuch as man is part of the cosmos, this applies also to him. But it is impossible that God, the final good that man as a spiritual nature ought "naturally" to attain, should be counted among the other good things that belong to man in the world. This *eros* towards God which is the deepest thing in man is not simply one love among others, even though superior to them, no more than God is a being among other beings. Today, when human reason exercises its inner-worldly function of ordering the world as never before, this must become self-evident, much more so than in some partly theological and certainly religious philosophizing as practised in the Middle Ages. Those who then spoke about the analogy of being always knew about the majesty of the "Altogether Other". Today this difference must be emphasized far more strongly, in order to prevent the analogy of being from appearing as one case among other analogies, hence as something which, after all, the human mind can master as one of its forms of thought. If it could do that, it could grasp and regulate the relation between God and man, hence dispose of the light that is given it by its own authority as if it belonged to it. The old Christian theologians knew why they placed the negative so emphatically above the positive theology, that is why they have always freed God and the "concept of God" from the clutches of rational understanding. The ultimate certainty is that I am not myself the Light. And this negation compels man to say "Thou" to the unknown, inscrutable Light, even though he does not meet this "Thou" as he meets the others; for this word remains a substitute to cover a mystery which, beyond all I and thou, has created both and preserves their relations.

What Schleiermacher so rightly called absolute dependence (*schlechthinige Abhängigkeit*) is only the other side of the primacy of negative theology, according to which free self-revelation must come from God, if another spirit is to know him. This should certainly make us very wary when talking about the analogy of being; for we ought always to remember that, as the human mind is the *a priori* of the knowledge of the world, so God and his self-revelation will always remain the *a priori* of the knowledge of himself. The inner-worldly experience of meeting persons will be the starting point from which modern man will define the relation of the finite to the infinite spirit religiously rather than philosophically, in the whole context of truth (*gesamtwahr-heitlich*) rather than merely theoretically, precisely because he has gained a clearer perception of the profane quality of theoretical reason. He must know that, however objective and precise his calculations, he will always have to account for his doings in the natural world from the point of view of man as a whole. He should know even more clearly that every theoretical formula of his relation to God (even the abstract one of the analogy of being) must correspond to his concrete spiritual relation to God, and that both relations must form a unity. Creating truth is an activity for which man is responsible to God, no matter whether it concerns the solitary individual, a team, a nation or all mankind.

It is true, today man's work is increasingly specialized, hence it seems as if the individual moved ever farther away from the centre of the synthesis and thus from the religious foundation of scientific and technical work and from the responsibility that should be behind it. Yet this is ultimately so only in appearance. For precisely this increased specialization gives the individual a share in the universal responsibility and thus an opportunity— whether open or hidden—to integrate his ethical and religious attitude into the whole, bringing the weight of his personality to bear on it. This weight he can only gain in his solitary relationship with God, in prayer and contemplation, in the risk of loving surrender to the ineffable mystery of our origin and ultimate destiny. But he cannot divorce these experiences from his daily life, relegating them to special occasions when he can leave behind all the degrading activities "the job" demands and at last once more be fully "himself". If he has really met God in that experience, this encounter will accompany him also into his everyday life; in fact, it demands this; it wants it to be also, indeed precisely, the day of the lowly human being who does servile work and cultivates this earth as a farmer or a technician or however else in the sweat of his brow and with a fundamental sense of ultimate frustration.

The leading spirits of our age warn us prophetically not to surrender ourselves completely to the technical craze, not to block the sources of contemplation. It is true, they are perhaps all tinged with a certain bitterness against the overwhelming power of the cynical, godless technical bustle. Heidegger's neologisms (*das Gestell*) aim at showing up spitefully its uprooted, ghostlike existence; Max Picard monotonously says "No" to everything, speaking from the perspective of the end, of the catastrophe of our modern ideal which he sees as present because it is inescapable. Bernanos angrily rejects all the modern lack of culture by which the beautiful image of man is debased and all high values are uprooted. Is there one who did not warn? There are, it is true, a few naïve churchmen enraptured by wireless, television and other aids to propaganda. Yet, apart from these, it is surely true that everyone who sells himself to these institutions for other reasons than having to live, has sunk below the mark in the estimation of all intellectual and spiritual people, that whoever accepts these developments without reservation can no longer be regarded as fully responsible. It is true, he must live; but he has sold himself, he has betrayed the mind to the machine.

The ideological superstructures erected above this reluctance of all contemplatives to "move with the times" are no longer important, such as, for example, the pessimistic attitudes following on Schopenhauer's philosophy of life, Spengler's morphology of culture and Scheler's dualistic gnosis. Today all these wrappings are shed, and what remains is simple anxiety for man. In view of the direction in which we are moving, the bare conscience of man responsible for himself is beginning to stir. Some imagine that they can already see the car rushing into the abyss and jump off, either by suicide or at least by categorically refusing to take any further responsibility. Nevertheless, everybody realizes that we cannot go "back to nature", as Rousseau naïvely imagined, nor shut our eyes, as the romantics did, with the exception of the one Eichendorff who saw what was coming and stood up to it. We have to find a mode of living with the monsters so that man can control them, and enforce his superiority to the robots, though it is certain to be an exacting task. But this superiority is not to be found where he is immediately tempted to seek it, namely in his technical genius which called them into being. On this plane the Marxist laws may largely remain valid. It can only be found on that other plane where the machine cannot penetrate. No machine has ever made the slightest contribution to prayer.

All those who are warning man today, do so from this point of view, in the name of prayer, contemplation and interiority, which are needed so that the soul may truly breathe and gather its creative powers, from which alone an external culture can fruitfully develop. Machines can only work upon existing mental achievements; and the treasures they use today belong almost entirely to the past. Will it be really good for Beethoven's symphonies to be squeezed for the thousandth time on old or new wavelengths, and to be pressed on to yet harder gramophone records? If the greatest works that have sprung from the highest spheres of the mind are to continue to bear fruit, they must constantly be drawn back into the highest sphere of those who receive them. Péguy writes in his *Clio*: "An honest, simple, reading done well is the true perfection of the text; it is, as it were, the crowning, like the frontal frieze on the column of a temple,

when maturity has been achieved. It is at the same time perfecting
nourishment and effect. . . . Here, perhaps, lies the deepest mystery
of events, my friend, the true mystery and the most interior
accomplishment in historical events, the secret of the power of
time. Our wicked, unworthy glances uncrown the temples.
A good, an antique view, fulfils; a wicked, a barbaric and modern
view dissolves. An unseeing, a nullifying glance, one that is no
glance at all, is in a certain sense the most wicked view,
for it is the view of final futility, of conclusive frigidity, the glance
of eternal rejection, lastly the glance of all destroying
oblivion. . . ." The glance of which Péguy here speaks must
not come from a less exalted and interior sphere of man than the
one from which the great works originally emerged. And this
has always been the sphere of prayer and contemplation—
analogously in the pagan, exactly so in the Christian, sphere. Only
the works of praying men have remained truly alive: Schütz,
Bach, Haydn and Mozart prayed, so did Giotto and Angelico,
Donatello, Michelangelo, Corneille, Racine, Pascal and Newton.
The humbugs who do not pray usually disappear in a few years'
time, to be replaced by other humbugs. And those who pray are
torn to pieces by the non-praying populace like Orpheus by the
Maenades, but even then they do not cease their music. Though it
may be abused so as gradually to lose its effect on the world, it is
preserved in a sacred shelter, where those who pray may easily
find it at any time. Before the dawn of the technical age it was
easier to create genuine culture from genuine recollection. Life
was more peaceful, man's surroundings expressed eternal values
more directly. Moreover, the requirements of average
education at school level did not overtax the intellectual capacities
of young people as they do today. All this cannot be left out of
account. How immediately a landscape from which men are
absent can unite us to God, for example high mountains, a large
forest or a freely-flowing river. The hand-writing of the Creator
can easily be read in them; even those who have forgotten how to
pray will once more learn, with deep joy, to listen to the sound of
the sources of existence. In the cities, however, only man's hand-
writing is everywhere visible, and much more so in the modern
than in the ancient ones that were still built according to human

measurements. Concrete and glass do not speak of God; they only point to man who is himself glorified in them. The cities do not transcend man, hence they do not guide to transcendence. Quickly and greedily they devour the surrounding countries and turn it into a dirty, defiled foreland of cities. For some years now the Roman Campagna has ceased to exist, the Swiss landscape likewise. The Rhine has long "had it". Overnight "nature" will be turned into a reservation; it will become a "national park" within the civilized world, and in national parks—mostly crowded—it is not very easy to pray either. If the works of the old culture always somehow derived from prayer and hence point to God, those of modern technical civilization do so no longer. They demand an attitude that seals off those sources that cannot be reduced to statistics; they require—even from the young, whose brains they usurp—a so-called "modern matter-of-factness" (*Sachlichkeit*) which becomes the prevalent state of mind. This invades almost automatically the metaphysical and religious spheres; but as it has nothing to do there and fails to achieve anything, it soon weans man from metaphysics and religion, from contemplation and converse with God.

The present time demands, indeed, a total anthropological attitude to the world in order to accomplish the total task imposed on it. Yet this same time is sick and decadent, and the opposition between the demand and the actuality is so overwhelming and mutually exclusive that the fulfilment seems to be deferred to the very distant future. Many, not to say most, within this technical world, have capitulated interiorly by giving up prayer. The Christians who are determined to persevere in it groan under the too great burden of external demands made on them if they want to compete with others who neither have nor allow time for prayer and thought. A synthesis between prayer and godless over-activity, between interior culture demanding a world of silence and external rush and ever increasing speed, becomes more and more an extraordinary attainment of the heroic few, and even so only for a limited time; it seems an impossible demand to make on a larger number of people.

This demonic situation cannot be mastered by desertion. Even in earlier ages it was dangerous for Christians to turn their back on the world of sense; today, when the practice of religion and Christianity is in danger of being considered as one specialized activity among others, this attitude is less permissible than ever. In fact, desertion is no longer possible today, when hermitages have ceased to exist and wireless and other amenities are penetrating even into convents, after having long been part of the normal life of presbyteries. But, if we share in the luxuries and useful equipment of our civilization, we also become its debtors, who may rightly be expected to take part in the common work. Those who refuse to do so become drones and are delivered over to the Marxian "process". This does not mean that, from the Christian point of view, pure contemplatives like Trappists, Carmelites and Carthusians have lost their right to exist in the modern world. They have only lost their right to desert; they remain members of the whole, functioning for it and vicariously effective in their action before God. Reinhold Schneider, following the best Catholic tradition, has described them as those who act most effectively in the world and its history, even though their action cannot—or can only accidentally—be verified. Today they are more necessary than ever, as they must be an example and incentive for all, exercising their effective function within the Body of the Church and of humanity. Others, spurred on by them, must themselves form islands of peace and contemplation through their own world of prayer; they must work on a higher level than the rest, convinced that these points of repose in the general rush are the most beneficial gift bestowed on man. Here the losses caused by being unable to keep up with the "competition" are far outweighed by the gains, since it remains true that the good of man cannot consist in his surrender to the machine.

For this very reason the religious man of today who knows about his freedom towards God must take care not to misrepresent the notion of responsibility. Man as spirit is above "nature" and even more above matter; he has become the free, authoritative administrator of the cosmic forces, dependent on the supreme Creator and Master of the world whom he represents, hence he is ultimately responsible not to the world and things, but to God. He pursues his worldly activities from an ultimate religious freedom which is the sole root of his responsibility. Hence human society cannot attempt to claim him for its common tasks by pointing to inner-worldly responsibilities based on exclusively social duties. Christians today like to assert that there is a conflict between the inner-worldly responsibility linked to the immanent laws of the things with which man has to do, and his religious responsibility to God. Such a conflict is by no means inevitable. Certainly, all we have said about modern man being linked to the body and the cosmos is valid. But all this holds good only if man is seen as man, that is as the being that has emerged above nature and looks up to God, not as the slave of sub-human forces. Seen according to the idea of this moment of the world's history (unfortunately not according to its factual reality), modern man's religious freedom ought to lead him to accept a religious responsibility for the world. It is not the world and its laws that compel him to do this; and Christians should beware of joining in this siren-song because they think it is up to date. Man himself decides to co-operate in free responsibility and free obedience to the Creator.

It should not be objected that in the modern world and its economic situation there simply is no choice but to howl with the wolves. The "necessity" that compels man to submit is ultimately (and decisively) founded not only on sociological and economic, but on religious factors. He is a man, that is appointed by God to be his image and likeness in the world and to administer creation as its master, hence he accepts the divine commission in the free dignity of his humanity. And he must continue to learn to be fully human until he succeeds in combining as best he can a stooping to matter with his gaze towards heaven.

If the scriptural account is true, man's working attitude that bends down to dust and soil is the punishment of his sin against God. Consequently, it is not to be expected that, even after his redemption by Christ, he will ever achieve a smoothly working synthesis of the two elements. Considered from this point of view, his work in the created world remains dialectical. Before the Fall he had been appointed to administer nature as its master; afterwards he is destined slavishly to serve the things he had wrongly turned into idols. The first vocation has not been abolished by the second, but it has been modified. Man is still a

king, but he is a humiliated king. Redeemed and brought home
by God, he retains his bent attitude, but his punishment is now
fruitful, at least in the heavenly sense. Still humbled by death and
suffering, the work he does co-operates, despite its vanity and
apparent futility, with the divine work of saving the world. The
meaning man has to create in the world can be valid only if the
highest and most interior sphere does not remain excluded from
it; the inner-worldly meaning must remain open to the transcendent meaning which is in God, and which God wills to mediate
to the world through man. This highest meaning will be fully
revealed to man only eschatologically; but it would be against
his spiritual dignity if God treated him only as an unconscious
instrument of this mediation. According to the analogy of
freedom and of being a person, he would also include man as
one who takes his part in the highest counsel, even though far
below planning Providence.

Why should not the rôle so explicitly attributed by the old
metaphysics to the angels be ascribed, with suitable modifications,
to man? Now the angels could only fulfil it because their objectivity was founded on the vision of God and they were willing,
in obedience, to accomplish every task. Thus in the case of man,
too, it is not indifferent in what degree he remains inclined
towards God, and how attentive his inner hearing is to God's
demands. It is true, God's plan for the world will not founder
even if man turns away from him and, in titanic revolt, seeks to
impress his own will on the world. In that case, providence would
necessarily have to take the form of a destroying judgment, which
is not the case as long as man submits to the eternal creation of
meaning in faith, prayer and obedience. Though he once lost this
capacity because he wanted to be like God, he has nevertheless
regained it in principle through the Redemption by divine grace.
The religious categories of turning away from and turning
towards God, of living according to the flesh and according to
the spirit, and the conversion from one to the other, do not only
influence the invisible "inner man", but through him his relation
to the world as a whole which, according to the explicit teaching
of St Paul, groans under the "aversion", waiting for the revelation
of the sons of God. Certainly, this will come about "eschatologic-

ally", because present existence as a whole is situated at the "turning point" from the old to the new aeon, from flesh to spirit, from disobedience and death to obedience and resurrection. Nevertheless, this *eschaton* will also reveal the true position of man in the world and the fruit that his service, performed in the world in obedience to his Creator, has produced even during this transitory time.

From this highest vantage point we shall be able better to see in their unity the three characteristics of man's present position in the world.

C. ANTHROPOLOGY AND RELIGION

1. *Man's encounter with himself as the crisis of natural religion*

THE change in man's position in the cosmos which we have shown, coincides with the historical phenomenon that the religious consciousness of mankind has been shaken in a way hitherto unknown. This was rightly seen by Comte, not only as regards the fact, which was not difficult to realize, but also in the inner connexion between the scientific and the—at first glance— irreligious character of the age.

Nietzsche's impassioned statement, "God is dead",[1] is really in the first place a statement, and not a war cry, considering the context and the language, which is one of sincere emotion. It is the statement that God is no longer alive in the world and in the hearts of men, at least not in the way he once was, according to Comte, in the first and second periods of history. Nietzsche realizes this fact with intense horror; for him it is linked to the sensation of absolute vertigo. He puts this on the lips of the "Madman" as a discovery of an event of incalculable consequences. For the time being it means a fall into the abyss, bound up with an icy cold, a putrid odour of the "corpse of God" and the ghostly activities of the gravediggers. Before Nietzsche, Feuerbach and Marx had expressed more soberly some of the things he announces in prophetic strain. Since then, we have become accustomed to much that was shocking to him and which has since become almost a commonplace.

[1] In *Fröhliche Wissenschaft* 125.

Nietzsche held Christianity especially responsible for the change in the attitude of mankind to God; in this he was followed by Berdyaev. In Nietzsche's view, the churches of today have become the tombs of God; living humanity races on its own roads past these monuments of its ancient piety without even wanting to find a relation to it. Christianity has made the world go atheist, by attracting to its own centre the piety diffused among the nations, the *logos spermatikos* of the fear of God that had existed everywhere in a naïve and unreflected form. Thus it has, as it were, absorbed the natural religious attitude of the world, integrating it into the only true supernatural religion of Jesus Christ. In his *Gods of Greece*, Schiller had already been forced to admit that the Renaissance had failed in its attempt to revive this naïve kind of religion in the Christian era. The concept of God has become a possession of the Church, in fact a speciality of the Christians who continued, indeed, to talk about natural religion, but interpreted it in the sense of a soul Christian by nature (*anima naturaliter christiana*). After the Reformation, this "Christian" interpretation had been narrowed still further into an "ecclesiastical" concept, so that the original universality of the notion could no longer be in any way kept up. The Christians, so it seems, have for so long insisted to the world that they alone have an absolute claim to religion that the world has tired of it and left the whole thing to them, an ecclesiastical speciality that has ceased to interest it.

Let us put this to the test and try to imagine St Paul's speech at Athens delivered in one of our modern capitals. "Men of Paris or Moscow", so it would have to run, "I find you in every respect religious. . . . What therefore you worship without knowing it, that I preach to you. God, who made the world and all things therein, being Lord of heaven and earth, dwelleth not in temples made with hands, neither is he served with men's hands, as though he heeded any thing, since it is he who giveth to all life and breath and all things." Today his opponents would not wait till he began to speak of the resurrection of Christ, when the old sages of Athens shook their heads, but would object at the very beginning of the speech, where Paul sought to connect the Gospel with the fact of natural religion. Since then something has changed. Surely some well instructed members of his audience would rise to tell him they objected to being called "in every way religious", a statement either made from ignorance or meant as an insult. They would further inform him that the whole passage about temples made with hands and human worship had nothing to do with them, but was instead very applicable to the Christians, who had turned their religion into precisely that for what Paul was blaming the pagans. But, worse than this, the whole address would somehow fall flat, for even those listeners who had not been trained specially in militant "cells" would hardly understand this point of departure.

What here looks at first like a neutral fact (whether it actually is we would leave open for the moment) has in recent times been interpreted in an opposite sense. The Vatican Council, not far distant in time from Nietzsche's outcry, has made the older position more precise by declaring "natural religion" a dogma of the Church. This is to say that in principle all men are capable of knowing God, though, since reason has been darkened by sin, it is also stated that the aid of supernatural revelation has become morally necessary. On the other hand, a different theology, such as that of Karl Barth, has turned the pretended "fact" into the contrary "dogma" of his teaching, stating that there neither is nor can or should be anything like a natural theology. What one might call the Christian and ultimately ecclesiastical restriction of natural theology to the revelation in Christ would, in this view, be only the discovery of the true situation that has always been valid, namely that natural theology in the sense of Nietzsche and Feuerbach has ever been idolatry, that is to say the self-deification of human reason.

Whatever the right interpretation, it is a fact that ancient and medieval Christianity has always talked to the non-Christian religions on a common basis. It is true, this was done controversially and apologetically, but within the sphere of a mutual understanding. There is the theory of the *logos spermatikos* of the first Christian apologists, which is then enlarged to the preparation of the Gospel, and later to the City of God that existed from the beginning of the world. This enabled the Fathers of the Church to adopt the method of taking over all the partial truths in paganism which found their fulfilment in Jesus Christ, the incarnate total Logos. In the case of the Jews it was anyway legitimate to take over their truths, since they had been entrusted with the Christian promises. Here we should not overlook two things: the Fathers do not distinguish between "nature" and "super-nature" in our modern technical sense; hence they could well regard the religious beliefs of the pagan nations as particles of a universal revelation that had always been both natural and super-natural. Consequently, they did not see Christianity in its denominational limitations but as the total world-religion—the *kat-holon*—into which the partial elements could be fitted after being suitably purged. This can be seen from the way in which sometimes even pagan myths are retained as reflecting Christian truth. Perhaps in the most grandiose manner this was once more done in the work of Calderon, and indeed in the whole of baroque literature and art: Christ is the true Orpheus, the true Odysseus, the true Eros who meets the human Psyche, and so forth.

In the Middle Ages, with St Thomas Aquinas, the attitude of Christianity to the world religions remained essentially the same. In the *Summa contra Gentiles* he once more conducts in the grand manner the conversation which Christendom had been accus-tomed to keep up with three partners: with paganism (from Plato to Aristotle), with Judaism (of the Old Covenant and its modern form in Moses Maimonides), and with the Islam of Avicenna and Averroes. In this conversation individual elements could be interchanged, while the one basis which united them all remained the same. For the first presupposition of all four religions was that man is not God, but can nevertheless be defined by his immediate relation to the absolute, to God, who does not belong to subhuman nature. Man is subject to fate, to providence; he is a being that must worship, even though something terrible and incomprehensible should happen to him. Ajax is a darker brother of Job; the *Prometheus* of Aeschylus a "religious" event, and not at all what German Idealism has made of it. Sophocles' *Oedipus* is almost a liturgical drama, as is also the *Antigone*. The man of Plato, but also the man of the dramatists and the Stoics, is a being that can and must be aware of the Divine; and this Christians on their part must also accept as a destiny, a dignity and a burden paganism naïvely experienced and accepted, before attempting any theological explanation. Man is indeed experienced as a "frontier" between this world and the world above, as one who cannot feel completely at home in the cosmos and is haunted by a longing to return to the Absolute.

Further, there is between the four partners in the conversation the common pattern of the bearer of revelation or the prophet. At the summit of the world there is one who reaches into the supernatural world and sees or hears heavenly things. Turned towards the heights, he is contemplative; and this enables him to be active when turning downward. The discussion bears on who this is: whether he is Moses in the cloud of Sinai, descending with the divine Tables, or Plato's king, the Poseidonic sage, Philo's prophet, Mohammed or, finally, Jesus Christ. Much that relates to this pattern has been handed on from one to the other so often that nobody knows whence came the first intuition. Thus it almost becomes a game between forms of thought. Dionysius announced the authentic Christian dogma in Platonic guise; Ramon Lull clothed the Christian teaching on love (in *Blanquerna*) in the trappings of Arab mystic Sufism; and Christian allegory could find and express its deepest mysteries in the Old Testament Canticle, indeed in all the writings of the Old Covenant. But the reverse way of thought was also possible. In his book on *Peace* and his *Sifting of the Alcoran* Nicholas of Cusa developed the vision of a Christian universalism for the last time before the Reformation, integrating the positive content of the other religions into the Christian fullness of truth.

The Christian partner in these conversations certainly did not overlook the darkening and hardening of Jews, pagans and Mohammedans which made it so difficult to talk to them, and which forced St Paul actually to speak of their being "without God in the world" (Eph. 2. 12) and of the frightful perversion of their religious beliefs into ridiculous idolatry and immorality (Rom. 1. 21). Nor would it have occurred to him to interpret that common basis as an exclusively "natural theology" in the modern sense. He did not leave out this factor, but rather included it in a very positive way. Yet beyond this he always envisaged a universal revelation of God guiding mankind as a whole, which nevertheless has its centre "in the dispensation of the fullness of time" (Eph. 1. 10). To the medieval mind Christianity is either a universal religious phenomenon or it is not. Christ, to whom had been given "all power in heaven and on earth", sent his disciples "to the ends of the earth". It is true, the Church is not simply the world; yet it is characteristic of antiquity and the Middle Ages that they would not develop a theology of the Church in the modern sense, though their concept of the Church was clearly defined from the political, social and canonical points of view. Nevertheless, it remained within the intellectual framework of the Augustinian theology of the City of God.

We need not here recount how this universal consciousness dissolved. It will suffice to mention the catastrophe in which the religious unity of Christendom broke up. For those outside, the "one Church" was replaced by many denominations, each of which, indeed, still proclaimed the Christian message, but could no longer do so with the same effectiveness. This happened at exactly the historical moment when humanity was becoming conscious of its unity, realizing first its geographical, and two centuries later also its historical unity, in which modern science includes also the cosmic prehistory of man.

The way in which Christian unity was so tragically replaced by the secularized world unity calls our attention to the fact that no smooth, organic transition could be expected. In his *Soulier de Satin* Claudel seems at first to envisage and glorify such a synthesis of the Christian and world unity from the point of view of the "Renaissance" (Day 2, Scene 5). But he soon corrects himself: in the Fourth Day the ideal becomes an illusion of the ageing hero, which he obstinately defends against his mystical daughter, Caritas (Scene 8), whereas, even before, the poet himself had affirmed the secret necessity of the inner rupture, at the beginning of the Third Day in the scene at Prague: "Of no saint has it been written that he was necessary, but Luther *had* to appear." In the Fourth Day, he recognizes the higher justice of the destruction of the Armada before the power of Elizabeth, and finally shows Christian unity to be transcendent, to be achieved only in repentance and death. Thus Claudel condemns not only the medieval reality, but also the illusion of the counter-Reformation, however much he emphasizes, on the other hand, the mission of Catholicism to the world, and even causes the angel to manipulate a revolving globe. Yet the Spain of the Baroque period did not succeed in uniting the world under Catholic auspices (according to the vision of Charles V in the First Day of the play and the enforced Faustian vision of Rodrigo in his American and Japanese expeditions). In the following century of the Enlightenment, the attempt to re-establish the unity under the banner of an artificially restored, pre-Christian, situation proved equally futile. The "natural religion" which had still been alive in the Middle Ages, strangely enough was no longer alive now, when it would have been the obvious substitute for the Christian religion which had become useless because it had split up into denominations. The French Revolution and its equally forced ideology suddenly illuminated the changed situation: the "Goddess Reason" was no longer the religious reason of the ancient Greeks; the *Etre suprême* had nothing in common with the *numen* of the old philosophers and dramatists.

But this was not due to the rational clarity of Christianity, as Schiller and his disciples believed, who held that, without its alien influence, the cosmic religion which it had destroyed would still be in existence. Barth is equally wide of the mark when he alleges that, since Christianity had shown up natural religion in its ghost-like unreality, even in its godlessness, the latter can no more be restored for this very reason. The true cause is otherwise. According to Berdyaev, Christianity made mankind aware of a transcendence of the spiritual which was no longer compatible with the organic and unquestioning religion of nature that had held sway until then. The Middle Ages still knew a sort of peaceful coexistence of both, and the modern development of secular consciousness cannot primarily be laid at the door of Christianity. It is true, this consciousness arises in the Christian nations and cannot be imagined without the "humanitarian" components of Christianity. For this conquers the national particularisms including that of the Jews, integrating them into the eschatological totality of the New Testament so lucidly described by Bergson. Besides, Christians are conscious of a vocation based on the explicit command to carry the Gospel to the ends of the earth, which have always been understood in a geographical as well as in a spiritual sense. But the main reason is the special character of Christianity that demands a decision. For Christianity links all religious belief inexorably to the affirmation of the divinity of a certain historical Man, and whatever refuses more or less explicitly this worship is, to begin with, rejected as irreligion (cf. the First Epistle of St John, but also St Paul's Epistles).

Yet all this remains latent until the day when mankind's interior consciousness and its natural historical growth have become sufficiently mature to be confronted with these dimensions of the Christian faith. It cannot be overlooked that this confrontation takes place in a twofold, hence equivocal, way: on the one hand, man takes over and reproduces the spiritual consciousness of unity in its secular counterpart; on the other, he sharply protests against the view that the former could become, or remain, the principle of the latter. The age of discoveries and of the beginning of a world-wide mission is also that of the Reformation. Therein the difference of the secular from the religious consciousness of unity is clearly defined: mankind, finding itself, does indeed understand that it would not have found itself without Christianity. On the other hand, it realizes that the true process of its reflexion on itself can take place only if it dissociates itself emphatically from the spiritual unity that has been given from above, and hence is eschatological and not immanent-historical.

Seen from the perspective of the Church, this second point presents indeed a dark picture: humanity unites under the banner of protest against Catholic unity. The Reformation is the religious signal that the way to this union is now free, but that it is therefore necessarily marked with the sign of Cain, the sign of rebellion and of protest. It is as if the inner unity of mankind's consciousness could not be envisaged otherwise than combined with the motto: "We will not have this man to reign over us." (Luke 19. 4.) Attempts to establish a new religious innocence miscarry, whether as a union of all men of (religious) good will under the banner of enlightenment, of Masonry (once approved by the greatest minds), or of liberalism, which contained the remains of a dissolved Christianity. Still, in the perspective of the Church, these failures to produce a modern natural religion appear as the judgment of the Christian God on the "modern" world that rejects and denies him. For the first time since the days of the early persecutions, the "world" once more takes on characteristically Johannine features.

It would be difficult to reject this manner of interpretation. But it must be supplemented by the more positive way of the first aspect, according to which the fact that mankind finds itself on the plane of its natural historical consciousness must be within the plan of providence. Nothing is more easily intelligible than that the age of particular nationalisms and imperialisms must give way to planetary unity, and that the new consciousness of humanity as a whole would appear as one that takes man as its starting point and common denominator. To this we must add what we have said about man being detached from the cosmic framework. His attitude to nature has changed; it is no longer experienced as the sheltering whole of which man is a "part": it is now the sphere from which man has ascended as regards his bodily being, and which he transcends because he is a spiritual being. Thus it becomes clear why the phenomenon of "natural religion" has been so badly shaken and has taken on such a questionable aspect in just this hour of history.

The existence of God as the "origin and end" of the world (as the Vatican Council describes it) is as immediately accessible and understandable to man as ever. But he stands before this God much less protected than in the age of cosmology. He can no longer afford those beautiful enthusiasms within nature which have so often provided an alibi for him, when he ought to have decided for or against the living God. They were states of mind in which even the majority of German Idealists were still entangled, who kept their spiritual world balanced between mystical piety and tragic atheism in a way that is incomprehensible to us today. What was really the position of Schiller, Fichte, Schelling and Hegel? Where did Friedrich Schlegel, Brentano and Görres stand in their youth, what is Hölderlin's pantheon from the religious point of view, and what does Novalis mean by the divine Ego? Where do we find here real prayer and authentic worship? And can even Goethe be excepted, if we think of his *Creed of the Parsee* and the tragic anthropology of his Pariah poem? True, he has reverence—but for whom and for what?

The God who confronts modern man can no longer be confused with gods and demons of nature. Man is a responsible spirit, hence God can only be the eternal Spirit who holds him responsible, and who is the Word demanding an answer. To this God man can only say wholly yes or no, he can no longer dally with him. Further, man as man, that is equally immediately as an individual and in community, is a responsible, adult spirit; he can no longer shelter behind a few leading personalities who are responsible for religion (cf. Dostoievsky's Grand Inquisitor), while himself behaving as an irresponsible kind of animal that just follows the herd. If he does so nevertheless, he has already made a negative choice; for today the herd that was once permissible no longer exists.[1] Christ's "flock" meant something organic that arose from, and was held together by the love between the Shepherd and his lambs; whereas Nietzsche's herd is a mass that can no longer be organically led but only ordered about. The "defection of the masses" is a tautology, even though it is a reality. The reaction that originated with Kierkegaard and his Catholic and Protestant disciples prescribed flight into the "individual", in whom the religious decision was to find its home. But this, too, has already been left behind, because the individual of today can only exist if he shares responsibility for the whole. Kierkegaard, Ebner and Haecker have spoken profoundly about the love of God, but in such a way as if the absolute religious passion isolated a man from his neighbour. They published another "Journal for Hermits" and seceded from their own epoch. This, however, meant abandoning the battlefield and leaving it to be occupied at once by the succeeding nihilism; and the escape itself is out of date, because a responsibility of the individual without community is no longer possible.

But this inter-relation of person and community in the religious decision is difficult to bear, the more so since the decision for or against God is today no longer a "private matter" but in the last

[1] The author here distinguishes between two meanings of the one German word *Herde*, where the English has the two different words "herd" and "flock". (Tr.)

resort a public affair, *res publica*. Therefore religion is nowadays so little in demand, natural religion is depopulated, and those who deny the whole phenomenon have an easy game. The "man in the street", too, has no difficulty. He can take refuge behind the scandal of Christendom: God has compromised himself with a denominational undertaking; the claim of the Christian Church to represent the unity of mankind's religious consciousness tending to God has been refuted and historically outdated by the multiplicity of denominations. Thus today, as never before in the history of mankind, the sanctuary appears defiled; the old reverence has been replaced by a cynicism of incredible dimensions, and the truly "natural" religion by a brazen irreligion that pretends to be just as natural.

Nevertheless, behind this crisis of natural religion there is something that must at least be regarded as a preliminary for a definitive relation of mankind to God, if not even as one of its inner components. This is the point in history when the consciousness of mankind (comprising that of every individual) has reached an immediate relation to the religious questions.[1] In the consciousness of pre-Reformation mankind things are compatible and simultaneously possible without presenting problems or dialectical tensions, in fact with a good conscience, which later are no more possible. This is not a problem of theology, but of philosophical sociology and psychology. Fèbvre sees very well that the unification of consciousness means two things at the same time: psychological "provincialism" or "federalism" is abrogated in favour of a thoroughly structural spiritual organization; and, paradoxically, the diffusive unity of Christendom is abrogated in favour of a sharply defined "confessional" Church. Unless we realize this, we shall commit the worst anachronisms; and we shall involuntarily testify that even the strictest *philosophia perennis* cannot neglect the historical dimension. The freedom of decision has touched the heart: the "Yes" or "No" is no longer spoken in secondary regions, while the central region is occupied by a general and natural form of religion. The discussion takes place in the very centre, where we can no longer even distinguish

[1]Cf. the important studies of Lucien Fèbvre, *Le problème de l'incroyance au 16e siècle* (Albin Michel, 1942), and *Autour de l'Heptaméron: Amour sacré, Amour profane* (Gallimard, 1944).

between what is private and what is public. This is so uncomfortable that mankind would prefer any other and earlier solution; yet there is no way back. This irruption of freedom into the secure natural regions is at first almost necessarily mistaken for an irruption of nihilism. The natural "Yes" to religion and through religion is suspended; otherwise, it would not survive the transition to freedom. In this pause of reflecting whether it is to be "Yes" or "No", many time-honoured certainties are suspended. This pause cannot be extended at will, because we are not free to decide whether we want to say "Yes" or "No" or not, only to make the decision at all. If a man does not want to say "Yes" he has already said "No". If he thinks it impossible to say "No", he has said "Yes", if not to the historical Christian revelation, which he may fail to understand, at least to a possible word from God and the obligation to obey it.

Hence we can also say that modern man's form of natural religion consists essentially in that he is a free "hearer of the Word" (Karl Rahner). He stands before the free, sovereign God, waiting to see whether he will reveal himself. Such a God is not "naturally" evident; if he is evident, even in his creation, it is only by reason of a sovereignly and personally decreed revelation (*apokalyptetai*: Rom. 1. 18). If this is to be understood and accepted (or refused) as such, it needs a human freedom that is capable of grasping absolute freedom. This concept of God is by no means the "projection" into the absolute of the human freedom that has reached its maturity, though the latter can be the condition of being able to conceive God in his sovereignty more adequately and absolutely. A growing vagueness and transcendence of the concept of God may be but a symptom indicating that this concept itself is growing among men.

Man has attained a new stage of his religious consciousness. In the age of cosmology he understood himself essentially as a "nature" with its natural ambitions, needs and desires. Then he inferred God from the character of his capacities and "tendrils" which were natural, even though opening into the infinite. Yet there lurked a suspicion, that could never be wholly silenced, that the God who was thus visualized and desired had, after all, to correspond to the measure of the human demand for happiness, truth or love. This is no longer the case; though this does not mean that the natural aspect of the creature is being denied. It is there, but it does not anticipate the ultimate fact, which is freedom. Hence the cosmos can no longer be understood so completely without a break as the Fathers and the Schoolmen, following Plotinus, saw it; that is as an effulgence of the divine sun of grace (the good is by nature diffusive of itself). Today it is marked far more profoundly by the abysmal incomprehensibility of the divine decision arising from infinite freedom.

Thus all three, God, man and the world, must lose something of their intelligibility. It is true, man still has a "nature", but this can no longer be defined as a closed, almost material (*sachhaft*) system of "capacities", but will become something that is open and will receive a form that may differ according as God calls and disposes. The "naturelessness" of man, so beloved by the existentialists, receives its sound religious meaning, without compelling us to give up anything of the natural knowledge of God defined by the Vatican Council.

Now it also becomes clear why the religious man of the Old Covenant who, in contrast with the Greeks, understood himself to be a hearer of the Word, had no reason to philosophize much about his nature. The object of his contemplation was rather God's dealings with his people, the past illumining the present and pointing as a promise to the future, while all three tenses revealed the nature of the God that was speaking. In such religious self-knowledge man becomes unknown to himself. But this is not a temporary state, as in the case of the things of nature, lasting till the knowledge has penetrated more deeply into his being, till the inner light in man has increased until it fills and illuminates the whole human space, so that knowledge extends as far as being. No, man is unknown to himself as only the "thing" man can be unknown, that is essentially and for ever, since man's meaning and vocation are buried in the freedom of God which, like a wall of fire, prevents any attempt to grasp them. But where God himself turns the face of his freedom towards man, he himself, too, cannot be seen. This is exactly the case with the God of the Old Covenant, whom man cannot see without dying, who forbids to make images of him and who shows himself only in darkness.

The last effect of this is that nature, too, created for man's sake, must be hidden together with him under the veil of invisibility and unintelligibility (*Unanschaulichkeit*). The fact that the cosmos has been rationalized by modern science would in itself be expected to produce the opposite result. Man receives the demiurgic power to arrange the world according to his plans and calculations. He gives it the face that he, as its master, expects from it; he fashions it into the comfortable home to dwell in. But just by treating nature in this superior way he deprives it of its natural face, as can easily be understood. First, things are made by God and not by man, hence they do not reveal their inmost aspect at his bidding, least of all if they are only pressed into his technical service. Further, if demiurgic man commands nature, he can only mirror into it his own lack of "face". Hence it follows that at the moment when philosophy turns decisively towards anthropology (at the end of the Middle Ages, and very clearly in Pascal) the face of the cosmos becomes veiled for man. Both events correspond to each other in such a way that we cannot say which aspect is the cause and which the effect.

Hence it is not enough to say that man has lost his sense of direction in modern nature, which has become unintelligible with its giant dimensions; that the house of the world has broken down and the wind of nothingness and "homelessness" blows through the ruins. We must also state the complementary truth: the dawn of the modern age is characterized by its own specific form of the spiritual and intellectual consciousness of mankind in general as well as of the individual, and in consequence of this gain, the mirror of the macrocosm in which man unconsciously mirrored himself was broken to pieces. Nature cannot be the adequate mirror of spirit, neither of the eternal divine Spirit nor of the creature, a spirit which, in its transcendence of nature, is an image of the divine Spirit. If today less than ever man thinks himself capable of defining and surveying the world, he has, indeed, added something to his knowledge of himself and of the world.

Man is no less religious because he has changed from a "mirror" into a "window", and no longer understands himself as reflecting the things of the world, finding himself encumbered with a multitude of objects. The religious situation, however, of the individual as well as of mankind as a whole, has also become less visible and intelligible, hence less suitable for external organization and doctrinal formulation. In the period of cosmology, religion, too, had an authentically cosmological form. It was firmly integrated into the ideologies of the old empires, it was a popular and state religion, a piece of the public order belonging to life in the same way as the authority of the sovereign, the traditions of the family and the solid framework of armies and economies. But though these empires often attained enormous dimensions, trying to spread over the whole world as known at the time, they remained interiorly "particular". None of them became conscious of humanity as a whole, each one of them ultimately established frontiers against some "barbarians" on its borders, where the world ended in the darkness of the unknown that could not be reached. The form of public religion, too, was bound up with this limited entity. But where the geographical unity of the globe becomes visible and the external world of men can be surveyed in its limits, there the inner unity of the consciousness of mankind develops (in the Reformation), which, contemplating this finiteness, can raise itself to the relative infiniteness of the spirit. From this moment, the cosmological form of religion becomes questionable. Man no longer recognizes in it the expression of his interiority which is open to God. The relativity necessarily bound up with these worldly, finite forms seems dull and repressive, incapable of containing and expressing transcendence. Religion disappears from public life; if it is still mentioned, this is done in a way as if it were almost something to be ashamed of. It is carried over from a former age into our own, but cannot be abolished because too many people still cling to it. In any case, it is something that demands to be officially tolerated, and hence must itself make toleration its supreme law and, if possible, even resign itself to its opposite, i.e. irreligion.

We are considering these things on the plane of "natural religion"; Christianity is left out of account for the moment; it will be discussed later. From this point of view the development cannot, at least not altogether, be considered a decline of religion. Indeed, if we seriously examine the consciousness of mankind as it enters the anthropological period, we cannot but expect such a disappearance of the finite forms into invisibility. The contemporary difficulty is this: the particular religious consciousness of the individual as the hearer of God's Word, who has to decide absolutely for or against God, can no longer be adequately separated from the social human consciousness as such. Yet the decision for or against God can only be made by individuals, and in the sphere of the invisible. Nevertheless, this decision is no longer a purely private one, but in a mysterious sense which is by no means clear, it envisages, represents and engages the whole. No one can strive for his own private salvation without considering his brethren, no one can want to separate his own destiny from that of mankind. If he did, his state of mind would certainly be anything but religious. And yet no one can credibly and effectively express this interrelated destiny of man and mankind. No one can make his own decision on behalf of his brethren, relieving all others from their obligation to make theirs. For at this stage, when religion has come to mean essentially this decision, everything depends on this, that each individual, representing the whole, should personally decide for God. Here we are at the actual centre of the "invisibility", which is felt by everyone, and which has become the great and sacred mystery of humanity's religion today. This mystery can no longer be adequately expressed by a public cult, as in the old pagan empires. Hence Christian moralists rightly assert that the pre-Christian state had exercised a providential, representative function in this matter, which was taken over by Christianity. As soon as this appears, as the true religion, promised and given by God (provided it actually is this), the state is relieved of its function of being responsible for the public cult which, in a Christian state, belongs to the Church. Hence Christians who seriously reflect on this matter will not unduly complain of the secularization of public life. And this is so not only because Christianity has relieved the state from the duty which it once legitimately performed, but because with the change of human consciousness this function can no longer be exercised—except by a religion that claims to be absolute.

2. *Contemporary natural religion and Christianity*

In the religious sphere, the unity of the consciousness of mankind cannot be expressed otherwise than as a question that is open towards what is above, that is to God. This question is so radical that it cannot even completely formulate itself: its character is intrinsically questionable. Man and mankind must decide for God as their Master, but they cannot do so as univocally as the nature of the case demands. The individual can decide, but he feels the paralysing weight of all those who have not, or differently, decided, and whom he yet ought to integrate and associate with his decision. Mankind is meant to decide, yet it cannot do so in the name of the individuals to whom the free decision must invariably be left. The slightest compulsion would at once, and rightly, be felt and opposed as "religious fascism".

Hence the consciousness of mankind in the anthropological period will revolt against a form of religion which, in the framework of a natural religious sense resulting from human nature, would claim an "absoluteness" other than this question that remains open to God, under which all other norms and theses of a natural religion would have to be subsumed. Indeed, the real character of our age as far as religion is concerned, will be found in the fact that all individual national and cultural religions can be made intelligible to the modern consciousness by this supreme openness: they are different forms of transcending towards God, which yet do not exclude an ultimate understanding of each other. It can definitely be regarded as religious progress that the individual forms become relative, even, or rather especially, if they include certain absolute factors which need to be analysed. Hence we have no objection in principle to investigating the phenomenology of the natural religions in the light of a total philosophical anthropology; if Jung's research is really this, if it does not deny all genuine transcendence by reducing it to purely psychological categories, it can be considered fruitful and necessary. The historical variety of situations and forms of expression must not be levelled down in a rationalist manner. For man's striving towards God is not a generic notion comprising a variety of different forms; it is always a question of each individual and his destiny, in which man, the problem creature of this world, confronts the absolute mystery.

It may be that the different forms religion has taken could be regarded as only relatively valid by the present age, in which the consciousness of mankind is becoming unified. All men are brothers in "Adam", all are burning with the same unanswered question; the deep understanding of the other, the stranger with whom one is in communion, relates nations and epochs. In this respect nineteenth-century historicism had an eminently religious undercurrent, as had the eighteenth-century Enlightenment. Seen from this point of view, toleration is more than a demand of cultural progress or a mere absence of enmity between views, rites and usages that exclude each other, though they have drawn more closely together. It is, in fact, the expression of man's metaphysical understanding of himself in this time. The question might be asked if the idea of toleration and the kindred one of human rights have come to prevail under the influence of (Catholic or Protestant) Christianity, or without it, or actually in opposition to it. Arguments might be adduced for each of these theories, each one may contain a partial truth. Indeed, humanitarianism cannot be conceived without a secularization of Christian charity. "Secularization" is a process which Christians normally feel to be ruin and defection, a "becoming worldly" in the sense of being profaned. Yet, even from the Christian point of view, it has its definitely positive aspect: it means that the Christian way of thought is accepted outside the sphere of the Church, that Christian postulates are recognized as true, and conclusions are accepted even without the premises from which they have historically been drawn, whether rightly or wrongly. The weight of the Christian impact contained in the conclusions that are accepted in the secular sphere may even be so great that those who agree to them without accepting the premises may yet, without hesitation, still call themselves "Christians". It is difficult to see that the Man who gave those ideas to mankind should himself have been God; but it is easy to understand that what he demanded was right, namely that men should love each other even to sacrificing their life, to affirming an ultimate solidarity in their final destiny. We might even admit that, strangely enough, mankind began fully to realize this just at the moment when the historical, religious and political unity of medieval Christianity began to dissolve. "So that by all means, whether by occasion or by truth, Christ be preached." (Phil. 1. 18.) It is already much if the nations obey the command of Christ, even though they reject the Church. For we shall be judged according to our deeds; and after all the prophecies of her Founder should make the Church expect only persecution and rejection. Surely it is the highest fulfilment of her mission if both be realized at the same time: her enduring mission of love, being allowed to sacrifice herself for mankind together with her head, and her teaching mission, blessed by grace, which, despite many particular failures, has yet had something like a world-wide success. Christianity, of course, can never be assessed exclusively as a historical fact. The visible aspect may deceive, the true records are to be found only in the book of God. Admittedly, secularization also means defection; men move away from the true source of light, the effect of the Church's radiation is diminished, her sacraments and blessings are lost. And, certainly, the growing uniformity of the consciousness of mankind can be "explained" also without Christianity, simply from immanent historical factors, though Christianity could be counted as one of these. This whole secularizing tendency has a clearly anti-Christian bias, just as the unity of the "natural" religion of mankind proposed by the Enlightenment and Idealism was unmistakably also opposed to Christianity, for what was to be "enlightened" was alleged to be confessional misunderstanding, not to say the clerical lie. This polemical element was a part of the development of mankind's unity, and it will remain as long as Christianity exists in its ecclesiastical form.

It will be much easier for secularism to become reconciled to those forms of Christianity that have broken away from the Catholic unity. We have only to think of Schleiermacher and Hegel and the whole world of sects and congregational churches of the Anglo-Saxon civilization: they are much more easily absorbed by the "world" than the Catholic form. And all these splinter forms of Christianity move irrevocably from one form of unity to the other: breaking away or being cast off from the one, they are attracted by the magnet of the other. They understand each other on the plane of humanity, they dissolve into liberalism and relativism. Even such a virulent form as Barthianism confesses openly that it would rather come to terms with Moscow than with Rome. Indeed, those Christian Churches that have broken away from Catholic unity more or less under protest, are the elements of the unity of mankind that are still nearest to the one Church, hence they show most clearly the polemical element of the former. It could probably even be shown that this Protestant migration from Catholic unity was the factor that contributed most effectively to forming the unity around the centre of the humanitarian idea, by which the Church's idea of unity was exported (and thus secularized) into the sphere of worldly culture, ethics and religion. The various forms of Protestantism must constantly justify their defection from Catholic unity both before themselves and before the world; hence they can only protest and dispute, else they would destroy themselves. Being forms of Christianity, they derive from the Catholic unity; they cannot deny their historical origin and turn away from it as from something that is finished once and for all. Since, on the other hand, they are non-Catholic forms of Christianity, the necessity of their defection from Catholic unity must always be included as a theme of their creed and their theology.

This borderline phenomenon between Church and world also combines the relatively strongest Christian content that passes over into the world with the strongest protest against what has been left; hence from this vantage point the relation between the two unities can be seen most clearly. For they are indeed two, and, today more than ever, this fact is the scandal of the Catholic Church. For, unlike any other religious phenomenon, she refuses to be subsumed under the unity of the problem of humanity. She will not be relativized; in the midst of time and history she makes her absolute claims. Those who are sympathetic to her try kind persuasion, while at the same time robbing her of all her riches which they themselves pretend to be able to use. Such are the treasures of her spirituality and mysticism (e.g. Otto, Nigg; and, I suggest, practically all High Anglican spiritual authors), of her external forms and cultural achievements (e.g. Maurras,

Schweitzer, ritualists and Anglican religious Orders); everything is taken from her, except that unbearable claim to absolute truth. With it she becomes ever more isolated, and soon she will be completely isolated and alone. For even Russia and the United States are only relatively opposed; if the political constellations shift, they may be reconciled overnight. The Far East does not confront the great powers with absolute demands, only with a more profound wisdom in answering the question "What is man?". The Catholic unity alone fails to fit into that of mankind. Until recently it had represented the principle of world unity; now, in the course of a few centuries, it seems to have become the antagonist, the spoil-sport that disturbs the peace of this unity. From one meeting to the next, the great Protestant ecumenical conferences dissolve greater tensions, digest greater divergencies, combining all shades of Christianity from the most liberal to the most orthodox. By doing this, they bring to light as never before the splendid isolation of the Catholic Church that separates her not only from all these brands of Christianity, but also from mankind as a whole with which all these are in contact. Even an understanding between the various Protestantisms and Russian orthodoxy is always possible, indeed largely under way. Thus it will ultimately be rather Protestant Christianity that is credited with having decisively fostered, or even actually formed, the unity of the world by its liberal all-embracing adaptability. It will become the cosmopolitan religion, in contrast with which the Catholic Church will appear provincial.

Yet this acute tension that has been brought about especially by Protestantism is only dramatizing anew an old situation that has always existed, which St Augustine had established in his *City of God* and his whole apologetic and polemical work. Modern theology expresses it by the formula: "Two perfect cities (or societies)", and thus opposes the two totalities in all finality. But just because natural theology has now taken on another form which is still growing, this encounter is not seen as a competition. It is the necessary form in which the highest eschatological unity the believer expects appears in history, a unity that only God can establish. The religion of humanity is ultimately the unity of the question put to God, the unity of transcending man (in which is certainly contained the transcendence of God himself as the beginning and end of the world). If this is true, this religion of mankind cannot wish to anticipate God's possible answer to this question. For it is just to the man who has become free that God appears as the absolutely and sovereignly free Being. And because man needs communication and intellectual exchange, he must be able to understand God as the eternal and absolute communication in himself (as the Triune Lover) who, if he deigns to speak, addresses mankind from his own initiative. If God has spoken, if he has given man a share in his divine life of communication and infinite love, then he has done it in a form which, being the most wonderful divine gift, brings the world at the same time the most improbable and unattainable answer to the question humanity has addressed to God.

As Creator, he has made man a creature that opens himself by asking questions, so that God himself may give him fulfilment in his revelation and redemption. The open question as formulated by the consciousness of contemporary humanity was the question of the unity between person and community, between the individual and the social decision for God, between the salvation of the individual and that of the "many" as Scripture expresses it. This question is founded in human nature which is necessarily both individual and social in Adam. It is impossible to leave out the social aspect from the most intimate religious decision of the individual; but it is equally impossible to burden the individual with the responsibility for the whole. (With this theory we really only repeat what St Anselm, e.g., presupposes in his theology of Redemption.) The answer to this question can only come from God. But it must at the same time be the answer of man and of mankind. The redeeming word must be spoken simultaneously from God to man and from man to God, and in such a way that the man who speaks it is quite definitely the individual, yet representative of the whole. It is intrinsically impossible that mankind should produce this representative out of itself; it cannot by a mysterious mutation pass from the stage of the uniform question to the stage of the answer that springs from this question. The unity of mankind's answer can only be an answer to God's word; a word of such sovereign freedom that it raises the liberty of the man who asks towards this supreme, transcendent freedom of the effective answer.

Considered after the event and in faith, Jesus Christ as the God-man is the most exact realization of what, in view of mankind's question, could be expected from God's free grace and mercy. He must be the messenger of the Father who comes from above to bring the Word of the Father; indeed to be himself the Word in his own existence. But he must also be the man who comes from Adam, in which the generations of men are summed up and who, being also from above, shifts the centre of human nature from the first Adam to the second which he is himself. Only thus will he be capable and competent to make the decision for God, which is impossible for man, both for himself and in principle for the others. This means that he takes upon himself the sin of those others who are turned away from God; he experiences their state of separation from God even to the abandonment of the Cross, but he does so voluntarily through love and obedience. The dark, mysterious tension which was present in the old Adam is not thereby rendered innocuous or destroyed, but redeemed; yet in such a way that the mystery continues and cannot simply be solved by reason. It has now become another tension. There is now Jesus Christ's redemptive decision for the Father, which has been made for all, and that of God the Father for Jesus Christ and all his brethren. But there is also the remaining necessity that the individual on his part must share this decision of Christ and God. It is not enough for man to side with the decision of God and Christ merely "by faith", to accept it and trust in it without on his part deciding for it with his whole freedom. The Protestant denominations incline towards this insufficient form. The Catholic Church demands that the human decision should be a visible and open profession, not only by words but by deeds. This follows necessarily from the fact that Christ is not only Man but also God, the eternal Son of the eternal Father. As such he is the new head of mankind, which cannot be identical with the unity of the natural-historical consciousness of mankind. No book, however holy, would have been sufficient to remind the world of this, nor any doctrinal teaching or mission, be they ever so exalted and zealous. Nothing but the unity that had been established in mankind by Jesus Christ himself could suffice, a unity which makes men conscious of the transcendence of the new centre in his name and with his guarantee.

The task which Christ thus leaves to his disciples is extremely precarious. It means that they themselves, as simple human beings, are to represent him, the God-man, among their fellows. They are bound to stand aloof from the general consciousness of mankind, not on account of their own talents and achievements, but only because of the faith and obedience entrusted to them. This attitude aroused the fury of the Roman emperors to such a degree that the Christians had to pay for it with their lives. And our contemporary intellectual pundits ask how the consciousness of mankind can tolerate this arrogance that contradicts all philosophy.

The consequence of such a perversion is . . . intolerance (i.e., to accept nothing but one's own statements that have been turned into dogmas) and the inability to communicate (being unable to listen to others and to be honestly called in question by them). Such instincts as will to power, cruelty and desire to destroy finally become motive forces that disguise themselves as such perverted will to truth. Then these instincts will find their more or less open satisfaction by pretending to serve the truth while indulging in a frightfully insincere self-justification. Nowhere except in the sphere of biblical religion does this exclusiveness of the adopted truth of faith seem to belong to faith itself, and is consciously proclaimed and pursued to its last consequences. . . . Even the New Testament attributes to Jesus, who offers no resistance and preaches the Sermon on the Mount, the words: "I have not come to bring peace, but a sword." There is the alternative to follow him or not to follow him: "He who is not for me is against me." The behaviour of many who believed in him conformed to this principle. According to the order of salvation as it presents itself to them, all those who have lived before or without Christ are lost. The many religions are a sum total of untruths or at best partial truths; all those who profess them are pagans. They ought to give up their religion and follow the Christian faith. The universal mission preaches this faith not only to all nations with all the means of propaganda, but it has always had at the back of its mind the will to enforce this faith where it is not accepted willingly. . . . The claim to rule the world is the consequence of the claim of absolute truth; in the great process of secularization—that is of retaining the biblical contents while discarding their religious form—even the fanaticism of unbelief is still influenced by its biblical origin. The secularized philosophy of the West often shows this trait of absolutism, persecuting other views, professing its own position aggressively, and subjecting that of others to an inquisitorial investigation. All this is done because everyone claims that the truth he represents is absolute. Consequently, philosophical faith can only resign itself to the unpalatable truth that, if communication is broken off and reason admitted only on certain conditions, the best will to open communication is powerless. I cannot understand how one can remain neutral when faced with such absolute claims.[1]

What Jaspers calls elsewhere the catholicity of reason shows itself ready to acknowledge and put up with everything except with the absolute claim which, shared in varying degree by the different forms of Christianity (also, to a less extent, by other religions), is maintained rigidly and irreducibly only by the Catholic Church. Jaspers speaks here as the typical representative of modern natural religion. He is fascinated by the unity of transcending reason that leaves everything open and neither desires, nor considers it *a priori* possible, that the question of transcendence can receive an answer from God. He therefore rejects *a priori* that form of religion which must claim to be this answer, even before its content could be examined or its claim justified, simply on account of its supposed presumption. Strangely enough, Jaspers' religious reason is so familiar with God that it can give him *a priori* prescriptions for every possible "religion within the limits of pure reason". This prescriptive reason which knows in advance that a revealed religion is impossible, in fact disrupts communication with God in order to confine communication to the human relationships of this world.

If transcendence to God (*Transzendenz zu Gott*) is to deserve

[1]Karl Jaspers, *Der philosophische Glaube*, Piper, 1948, 72–73.

its name it must remain expectantly open not only to man, but especially also to God, waiting to see whether he will speak a divine Word in history, which could then sound simultaneously both above history and within it. It would have to do so in history, because otherwise men could not hear it at all; but it would be heard in such a way that God's claim that man should listen to him above all others would seem both intelligible and justified to human reason. Whoever knows human nature will not be surprised if those who are called to proclaim this demand of God before history are likely not only to be misjudged from without, but also to abuse the task entrusted to them. Here *a priori* considerations are certainly not out of place. The idea of a possible Church, therefore, includes also this contingency. Since it must necessarily consist of sinful and guilty men, it will not be entirely the fault of those outside if it becomes a scandal to them. And even though this point of view will remain valid until the end of history, we ought not to overlook one fact: the temptation of applying external force which Jaspers singles out for his special censures was conditioned to a considerable degree by the stage the consciousness of mankind had reached at the time when this happened. In those days mankind was very far from thinking this an abuse of Christ's commission; on the contrary, it considered it a permissible, indeed an appropriate, form of carrying it out, and approached the Church on its own account, that is through the State, with the requisite demands. The State called on the bishops to become counsellors of the realm and made them secular princes; secular rulers ordered compulsory baptisms, kings, not Popes, introduced the Inquisition and lit the stakes; secular army chiefs have the atrocities of the Age of the *Conquistadores* on their conscience. Certainly, the approbation of the Church was always sought, and the representatives of the Church who were so closely united to the secular powers could be persuaded to share the responsibility. Nevertheless, since the Reformation, Church and State have grown more and more apart, and, according to Jaspers, fanaticism has come to the fore especially in the secular sphere, even though he maintains that it is an after-effect of the Christian period. Yet we would rather draw the opposite conclusion: even then the abuses originated chiefly in the secular sphere. Today no one can hold the Church responsible for the concentration camps of the Nazis or the Communists.

It is also important to stress that the attempts to divorce Jesus from the Church are being gradually abandoned. Even a short time ago it used to be the fashion to see in Jesus the type of the religious genius who draws men's attention to the heavenly Father in whose sight all are brothers. Those were the golden days of Renan and Harnack. One could, at most, see in Jesus the last of the Jewish prophets; yet though Martin Buber joins liberal biblical criticism and splits up the Gospel into a primitive Jewish nucleus and later Pauline and Johannine additions, he is wise enough to admit that even the historical Christ cannot be acquitted of having made absolute claims. In order to save Renan's idea for mankind attempts can, and always will, be made to go behind the offensive absolute Christianity, though this is already the religion of the primitive community, and to grope for an "X", which may be indicated extremely indirectly in the earliest texts. It might just as well be admitted at once that the historical Jesus such as we know him cannot be brought into line with the modern humanitarian ideal. He would have to be relativized in the same way as the other religions, which means that he would have to be understood better than he understood himself. One will then try to take up some intermediary position on the slippery tightrope between orthodoxy and liberalism, on which ambiguous theories are precariously balanced (like that of Bultmann, for example); but this procedure is, obviously, quite arbitrary.

We would not, however, deny that it is dangerous, from the sociological point of view, for the Catholic Church to be thus isolated as the only religion which, in the coming age, will still claim "absoluteness" in the sense of universal validity. The danger can lie in two directions. Since it is a well-known fact that the herd-man is afraid of getting mixed up with the "party" of an isolated minority that is likely, and even certain, to be attacked, a progressive "defection of the masses" from the Church can be prophesied with corresponding certainty. The persistent protagonists of the "category of the individual" will be pleased with this; the Church as the Mother of men, commissioned by Christ to feed his flock, cannot take this attitude. She will look for ways to reach once more the mass of mankind, and perhaps adapt her ways and means somehow to those of the world. She may perhaps instruct her members more emphatically on the nature of her authority, just as on Sunday the parish priest may reproach the small congregation that still comes to church for the sins of those who have stayed away.

These are dangers, but they are not fatal if the divine Spirit who guards the Church and her obedience to her commission continues to protect her in the age of the "little flock". The man who belongs to the Church, however, will himself have to avoid everything that could smack of isolationism. This might be caused by a reaction of fear, which withdraws, perhaps still fostering romantically the forms of former world-power which have now become outdated. It may also be due to a sulking attitude which, afraid of further insult, prefers to stay at home, or to exaggerated traditionalism which neglects the man of today and tomorrow in its enthusiasm for a magnificent ecclesiastical past. On the contrary, when representing Jesus Christ—whether this is done by members of the hierarchy or by simple laymen— it is always of crucial importance to keep the spirit of universalism, and to avoid that of particularism and opposition.

The Catholic will have to be on his guard against a certain negative phenomenon in the consciousness of humanity. As has already been said, mankind only becomes conscious of its unity in breaking loose from, and protesting against, the claims of the Church to be the religious form of unity willed by God. This protest is wider than Protestantism in the narrow sense, but gives it some affinity with the other religions of mankind, and so is bound to lead to a kind of *entente cordiale* between all non-Catholic forms of religion. "Anything but this" is the common watchword by which all non-Catholics easily understand each other. In this understanding all absolute factors are gradually levelled down; the only exception at present is the rigid dogmatism of the Communists. Hence the religion of humanitarianism can ultimately be no better recommended and demonstrated in its inner spirit than by contrasting it with Catholicism. There is no slogan nearly so suitable for all forms of modern cultural propaganda as that which promises to lead men from Catholic "narrowness" into the "breadth" of natural religion. The world-wide unity of the religions is being hammered out on the anvil of Catholicism. It is enough to study attentively the repertory of any modern theatre. Most "Catholic plays" are well suited (that is why they are popular) to make the non-Catholic public shudder at Catholic absolutism (Bernanos, Claudel, Reinhold Schneider, down to Hochwaelder and the "First Legion"). On the other hand, most other plays dealing with some religious problem blow up this world of terror from within; we may think of the properly Jasperian "communication" between Shaw's Joan and her Dauphin. It has long enough been the fault of Catholic poets to let themselves be driven into the Kierkegaardian opposition of the individual. We need modern poets open to the world like Claudel, but able to depict even more vividly the glory of the Christian life.

What holds good for poetry and for every form of art and culture is ultimately valid for the whole Christian life: the Church is not a secondary factor, on a par with the consciousness of mankind. This would be absurd and imply a schizophrenic condition. The Church has to represent this central event in the world: that God has spoken his Word in answer to the question man and mankind had put to him. This Word was an atoning and redeeming Word, in fact a grace, which shows itself as such precisely in this, that it is no longer transcendently spoken down from heaven, but has become flesh and, dwelling among us, has deigned to become a new centre for the consciousness of mankind.

Hence there is no essential dualism between the consciousness of the First and the Second Adam, but the unity of a change that is happening, of an event that takes place by grace in this consciousness, immensely enriching man's relation to God. Nevertheless, this event that has taken place once and for all in the centre of time, is yet ever renewed for every man and for each generation, and will wholly be accomplished only at the end of the world. But the Christian has the duty to live in the heart of mankind, keeping in view both this turning point of the Incarnation and its eschatological fulfilment; and he must do this not by separating the spheres of the old and the new Adam, but by uniting them in himself.

The modern concept of the world has become dim and hard to discern, because man is more than the world, and hence the old correspondence between the macrocosm and the microcosm is no longer valid. This "being more" is dynamic, in so far as, on principle, no closed view of the world can catch up with the openness of the spirit that surpasses the world. The dynamism of this "more" is only received into the dynamism of the Christian "more", which is the "ever more" of God's infinity in regard to man. And yet, between God and man all is not resolved into a limitless dynamism. There is an exact correspondence between the infinite and the finite spirit: Jesus Christ, God and man, two "natures" in one "Person", Son of the Father in heaven, son of man on earth, who transmits and inscribes his divine Sonship into the "form of man", who is the eternal Word of the Father and at the same time keeps this word on earth unto death. Thus he is true to himself and at the same time corresponds both to God and to man.

Because man as such is the *locus* of being in the world, he is unlimited and open towards Being. Thus he cannot be fully made into an object. It is possible to investigate all the aspects of man that are the subjects of individual sciences. Yet this can be done with the right *a priori* and promise some success only if one refrains at the same time from interpreting man according to a consistent idea, however sublime. For man is the image of God, of whom it is absolutely certain that he cannot be defined by any finite formula. If you understand him, he is not God. This much philosophy is able to state. But the unknown God comes alive for man by revealing himself, and so the unknown creature, man, also becomes important and fascinating in his incomprehensibility. His features come to life, are lit up and deepened, when man beholds not his mirror but his original. Only in the triune unity of God does man's unity appear and find itself, as he turns from the old Adam to the new.

II

RELIGION AND CHRISTIANITY

THE SECOND part of this treatise is closely connected with the
first. We now presuppose the historical explanations that have
there been given and assume that the religious situation of modern
man and the form his natural religious sense has taken have
become fairly clear. The impression this religious situation as a
whole leaves after a first survey is one of withdrawal, of im-
poverishment, not to say of actual indigence. The old views and
customs hallowed by habit have become empty and meaningless.
We shall have to guard against taking this impression for final,
and especially against regarding it as either wholly negative or
positive, as the case may be. Structural changes in the history of
the human spirit normally have a neutral aspect: they may be
interpreted in different ways; above all, man may make of them
this or that in a given situation. It is especially the duty of
Christians to bring this creative touch to the spiritual "material"
a period offers. It is part of their vocation to interpret the times,
according to the world of Christ: "You hypocrites, you know
how to discern the face of the heaven and of the earth: but how
is it that you do not discern this time?" (Luke 12. 56), further,
they must give a Christian shape to whatever the time offers.

Modern art may be taken as an example. The Victorian age
was followed by Edwardianism, when ugly and beautiful things
were produced side by side. This, in its turn, gave way to modern
simplicity which first expressed itself in a wholesale rejection of
ornament. Was this due to incompetence, or to a longing for
purity of form, line and space? We all know that it can be due
to either. It may express the spiritual dearth of the modern machine
world which can invade any home and any branch of art, or it
may be a welcome return to true simplicity and good taste. It is
always the question of what kind of personality and ability a
man brings to the prevailing style.

Thus the contemporary concept of God, too, has a style, which the Christian ought to recognize and in which he ought to express himself. And he should do this not only from without, diplomatically and apologetically, but from within: as a child of the age who shares its situation, its needs and abundance, and who yet knows to draw from the treasure of God's revelation entrusted to him "new things and old" (Matt. 13.52). By interpreting them rightly he will help both himself and his time.

A. THE UNKNOWN GOD

1. *The hiddenness of God in our time*

NOT only the Christian God, but the God of natural religion is hardly ever mentioned by modern men. The men of the Enlightenment used his name so frequently as to be almost irreverent. Whenever it happens to occur in a modern newspaper or a speech it sounds mostly false and empty. Human respect may be one reason, but also a shyness to call God at all by his old, well-known name. It is as if everybody knew him and were familiar with him, as if he were a being to be treated as one among others, admittedly a Supreme Being distinguished by his position at the summit of beings, but only a *primus inter pares*.

Time and again a generation seemed to be pious and God-fearing if it left in the world gaps which, it was alleged, could be occupied only by God. Yet these would always close, and yet another opportunity was lost for pointing to God and touching him with one's hands. More and more honours and privileges that men had reserved for the First Cause fell to secondary causes. And thus ever more things that seemed to be "known" of God had to be referred to the world. This is the essence of the whole historical process described in the first part, the conquest of the open or hidden religious cosmologism by anthropologism. Even while modern science was carrying all before it, the defenders of the idea of *Deus sive natura*, attempted a cosmological counter-movement, and ventured to make God visible and accessible by man. The Idealists even went so far as to attempt to build up the inner being and consciousness of God from nature and the human spirit. Compared with this outrageous irreverence, Goethe was a man of reverence; yet he, too, saw in nature the "sacredly public mystery" of God, and recognized the essence by its coloured reflexion, "for it is the eternally One that reveals itself in manifold ways". The modern heirs of German Idealism have lost Goethe's ingenuous accents and moved away from the natural centre to the borders of sectarianism. The Goethe of Rudolf Steiner is certainly not Goethe, and the cosmological Eros of Ludwig Klages is not that of his great poems. The "becoming God" that appears sporadically in Rilke's poems is a miserable spectre; and Kerényi's literary heaven of the gods has only the name in common with the classical original.

The world is not God. This much is clear today, to the theist as well as to the atheist. Nor is the world open to God in such a way that he would have to intervene in it at every moment to keep it going. We do not add to the greatness of the Creator if the Prime Mover is called in wherever we notice a gap in the secondary causes. Christian apologetics has probably by now learned from its past mistakes; its history, especially at the end of the nineteenth century, resembles a chain of well-meaning mis-understandings followed by enforced retreats. Today we see clearly that we cannot fight science with Scripture, because the aim of God's revelation in the Bible is not to teach men science. But how dearly had this understanding to be paid for! Perhaps something similar is happening now with the temporary difficul-ties of the modern science of the world. Surely Christians should help to solve and integrate them instead of constantly finding occasion to postulate an immediate intervention of the Creator, who, they think, shows himself in this way. It seems that the world is an expanding system, which therefore could be traced back to the moment of its origin. Surely a proof of God's creative action, cry the apologists. Perhaps. But perhaps St Thomas Aquinas was more profoundly right in his view that the beginning of the world cannot be proved by mere reason. The material world contains elements of indetermination. This, it is alleged, is a proof *a fortiori* for the freedom of the spirit, as if these were not two quite different phenomena. The discussion of the view that life cannot be derived from matter continues; but this could only be assumed if matter did not contain the principles of life from the beginning. It is the same with the discussion of the development of mind from life below mind. This would indeed be unacceptable only if the idea governing the development of life were not from the beginning the idea of man. In all these cases the purely evolutionist view would always be only one side of the truth. The great leaps of nature from one stage of being to another may be facts; yet this does not prove at all that their explanation requires a supernatural cause.

If contemporary men are here instinctively mistrustful and cautious, they cannot be blamed if they are also more reserved than former generations with regard to the Christian accounts of miracles. The Middle Ages, especially at the end, had a real mania for miracles. But the seventeenth century was the same, as is proved by its hagiography, and the Romantics, too, in their own way, mixing up miracles with their cosmological occultism. What a Görres, a Brentano and most of their like-minded contemporaries have produced in this field seems truly frightening to us. Yet even nineteenth-century France had quite a naïve attitude to miracles; we may think of Léon Bloy's story of Mélanie and of so many strange happenings at places of pilgrimage which ultimately remain shrouded in an obscurity that cannot now be penetrated. Things that are completely clear to a small circle within the sphere of the grace received need not be equally so for everyone else. The investigations of the limits within which occult and parapsychological factors operate within the created world are only in their infancy. The material will be immensely enlarged by Oriental, especially Indian, data. Many a judgment that at first seemed assured would better be received with reserve. Christian apologetics itself has rightly modified its views on the Scriptural miracles. The full force of argument, especially as regards the miracles of Jesus, is now seen to consist in their connexion with the phenomenon of Jesus himself. They are not isolated magical feats, but emphasize just this and no other word, this doctrine, this witness, this existence. Jesus himself always points to this connexion. The miracles draw men's attention to his words and existence; the "works" are meant to facilitate this access, and, since the words of Jesus are worthy of credence, his miracles must be so, too. The progress that leads from them to faith is proved legitimate—from the point of view of faith. The same holds good for the Old Testament prophecies. They, too, are not to be taken as bare philological statements, but must be seen in their historical setting; they point forward to Christ as the Messias and find their fulfilment in him.

All these apparent retreats are not signs of scepticism or rationalism, but are caused by the legitimate caution of religious reason, to which it has become increasingly clear that the First Cause is transcendent.

> God is not a piece of the world, but its presupposition. He is not an objective piece of knowledge beside other objects, but the infinity that is always presented in advance to the movement of knowledge, and within which the latter pursues its courses which will always remain finite. God is not the concluding hypothesis that follows from the preliminary sketch of a perfected conception of the world, but the only thesis that is posited with every one of the hypotheses from which we build up our concept of the world. . . . The world has become an entity rounded off in itself, which is neither actually open at certain points where it merges into God, nor undergoes at certain observable points the causal impact (*ursächlichen Stoss*) of God (if we disregard for the moment the supernatural dispensation of salvation); but it points to God as its presupposition only as a whole, and even so not very obviously. Today man realizes that this is so, having gradually acquired a scientific concept of the world that is just as profane as the world itself, which is not God. . . . We are experiencing today that we can make no image of God that is not carved from the wood of this world. The educated man of our time has the duty, painful though fruitful, to accept this experience. He is not to suppress it by a facile, anthropomorphic "belief in God", but interpret it correctly, realizing that, in fact, it has nothing in common with atheism.[1]

Nevertheless, the non-Christian can hardly interpret the signs of the times other than in terms of atheism. This is clear not only

[1]Karl Rahner, "Wissenschaft als Konfession?" in *Wort und Wahrheit*, IX, November, 1954, 811-813.

from its organized mass appearance, but also from the reasons
we have explained. Political and materialistic atheism is, in a
more profound view, only the popular historical consequence of a
historical necessity. At one time, God's nearness had been felt in
nature, in the whole visible cosmos which on its borders merged
almost without break into the invisible sphere of the divine. This
is no longer so either, emotionally or intellectually.

> Men are frightened at the absence of God from the world, they
> feel that they can no longer realize the Divine, they are terrified
> at God's silence, at his withdrawal into his own inaccessibility.
> The world becomes profane and devoid of meaning, its laws
> are impersonally objective, even where it is no more a question
> of nature but of man. This experience which men think they
> must interpret theoretically as atheism, is yet a genuine experi-
> ence of the most profound existence . . ., with which popular
> Christian thought and speech will not have finished for a long
> time. But it is fundamentally only the experience that God does
> not belong to the concept of the world; . . . it means that God
> is growing in the mind of mankind. We experience anew and
> most radically what we, and the Vatican Council, have always
> known theoretically, but have said somewhat unthinkingly:
> that God is ineffably above all else that exists and can be
> conceived.[1]

The sentence with which the Council begins[2] is the foundation
of all its later statements on natural theology. Surely it is not surprising that this first sentence should become more topical than
ever at a time when the cosmological conception of the world is
changing into a predominantly anthropological one. As we shall
see, it has never been unknown to Christian theology. All truths
have their particular hour; and this truth has its hour today.
Christian theology and spirituality will perhaps be terrified to
realize that they have not been quite prepared for this. The reason
is that this great insight into the divine Being, which so completely filled the heart and mind of the Fathers and the medieval
mystics, has not remained equally alive in the last centuries. Seen
from this point of view, the frightening phenomenon of modern
atheism may, among other things, be a forcible measure of

[1]*Ibid.*, 812.   [2]Denzinger, 1782.

Providence to bring back mankind, and especially Christendom, to a more adequate idea of God. The anti-Christian virulence of this atheism cannot be answered by a corresponding "anti" of the Christians. The Christian answer must know how to hold up the blind, hostile stroke in the depth, and to change it into something that brings light and unity.

2. The Christian idea of the transcendent God

In late antiquity, when Christianity made its appearance, one can notice a similar disappearance of God into an inaccessible transcendence, though in a lesser degree, and with this difference that the Neo-Platonists recognized the essence of Divinity in this transcendence. Nevertheless, this religion was of an abstractness and partly of an intellectual eccentricity that have a certain kinship with the modern frigidity of mind.

The Christian answer is by no means confined to stressing God's visibility in his economy of salvation, in his nearness to men in the Incarnation, in the apparitions and voice of the Old, the sacraments and graces of the New, Testament. On the contrary, the Patristic doctrine of God lives by, and gains its depth from, the great breathing space of the negative ("apophatic") theology, which the Fathers regard as the crowning of all human thought about God. In this they are in harmony with the philosophers, though they move in a different spiritual atmosphere. The Cappadocians, for example, reject inexorably the rationalism of the Eunomians, according to which it is possible to form a concept (*katalepsis*) of God, by stressing that God can ultimately be "grasped" only in so far as man knows he fails to grasp him. What he grasps, says Gregory of Nyssa, he also dominates; but the mind can only be dominated by God; it experiences something of the reality of its Master when it abandons its claims to rule. In having to resign itself to not knowing *what* God is, the failing spirit divines *that* he is; and this "Is" can therefore not be added to that of the creatures, but shows itself as the altogether Other and Greater than all in the failing of all images and notions. This is the teaching not only of those Fathers who were influenced by Alexandrine and Platonic thought down to its great representatives, Dionysius and Maximus the Confessor; the same was taught by the realistic Chrysostom, whose homilies show their true character only against this background, and by Novatian, from whom we should like to quote a few sentences by way of example:

> The human mind is incapable of thinking adequately about God and his essential attributes, what he is, how great he is and in what manner he exists. Nor can the art of human speech develop an eloquence proportionate to his majesty, for he is greater than the mind itself and cannot be thought as great as he is, so that he should not, when he is being thought, be smaller than the human mind that comprehends him. He is above every word and ineffable, so that, being capable of being expressed, he may not be less than the human assertion which could circumscribe and gather him into itself. Whatever can be thought of him is less than he, and whatever can be predicated of him is smaller if compared with him. For we may, indeed, feel him a little in silence, but we cannot express in words what he is himself. If you call him Light, you name a creature rather than himself, you have not expressed him. If you call him Force, you describe his power rather than himself. If you call him Majesty, you express his honour rather than him. Why go into detail? I will say it once and for all: Whatever you say about him, you have explained only something that belongs to him, one manifestation of him, not himself. Unless our intellect might grasp in one unique way what God is—but even that: how could we do it? How could we comprehend it? How might we understand it?—namely by imagining that he is that which cannot be understood or even thought in its intrinsic greatness . . . God is that which has the property that nothing can be compared with him.[1]

The great "articulation" is between theology (God in himself, exalted above all) and economy (God for us, in his grace condescending from his infinite superiority). But the economy or *syncatabasis* (concession by grace, descending below oneself by way of adaptation) can only be measured in its full character of being a grace if, at every moment of it and in all its manifestations,

[1] *Liber de Trinitate*, Migne, PL 3, 889–891.

it always remains clear who it is that condescends and adapts himself, who is making such concessions to the creature as to deign to meet it and be known by it. Thus a true "economy" is possible only if it is constantly balanced by "theology". The Father sends the Son, and the visibility of the Son must point to the invisibility of the Father with all the available means, positive or negative. Hence, within the economy, nothing must be isolated from the background of the ineffable that can only be adored though understanding fails; nothing is to be taken, worked up and rationalized by itself in order to be opened towards infinity, and only then, in a second stage, to ascend from the "literal" to the "spiritual" sense. Nothing can be understood of the humanity of the Son if it is not from the beginning experienced, believed and adored as the humanity of the Son of the *Father*. In no word of Christ and of the Bible can there first be stated an immanent content valid in itself, which would then, afterwards, be opened into the depth of the divine meaning. Because the Fathers, especially those influenced by Origen, attach such importance to the resurrection and ascension of the Son, their Christology does not become a one-sided theology of glory, but simply a real *theology*. For in this everything depends on the angle that opens from the finite to the infinite, on the gesture of adoration before the mystery which is accomplished ever new in the theological act.

The Fathers worked on this golden background. They had the feeling for the dialectic of that which is always greater. Just because the angels are so near to God, says Chrysostom, they understand better the divine incomprehensibility. And he who knows about God's incomprehensibility knows more than the man who does know about it.[1] We have the same emphasis in Augustine, and again in the Middle Ages in Abelard, Eckhart and Nicholas of Cusa. St Thomas Aquinas wrote frequently to the same effect. A late work such as the *Commentary on Boethius* is the exact echo of the teaching of the Fathers. He also knew that it is impossible to have an idea, properly so called, of Being, even though everything is known only in its light.

But what has become of this emphasis in recent times? It is

[1]*Peri akatalepton*, Migne, PG 59, 721, 742.

there in Ignatius, in the *Ascent of Mount Carmel* of John of the Cross, and in Erich Przywara. But has it still the same effect as formerly? Does it shape the life of Christians, does it influence the sermons of preachers or the thought of theologians? Or has this golden background been damaged and broken, left unrepaired? Are not most people content to worship undialectically God's appearances in the world, to stop short at the visible Son, at his Mother, at the Sacraments, without vitally realizing the dynamisms which this whole world of appearances receives from the invisible Father and impel it towards him? Surely St John would not have loved the Lord if in him, who could be seen, heard and touched, there had not appeared the Word of Life, reposing in the bosom of him whom no one has ever seen? And would St Paul have surrendered himself to him, if he had not been the epiphany of him "who only hath immortality and inhabiteth light inaccessible; whom no man hath seen, nor can see"? (1 Tim. 6. 16.) Are we the disciples of these men? Or have we not rather, since the Counter-Reformation, clung increasingly to the visible? Perhaps we did so thinking this had to be defended against the spiritualists, and thus, as Henri de Lubac has rightly pointed out, we have begun in these last decades to abuse the conception of the Incarnation for the sake of our earthly interests and conveniences. We settle down in the visible, excusing ourselves with the earthly mission of Christians, with the modern mind that is turned towards the world, and with the Greek infiltrations in early Christian thought. We have been incapable of sacrificing the world to God. A simple Buddhist advances much farther in this respect. Surely it is time for God to show us the aspect of his infinity, his "altogether-otherness".

Only those Christians who are most deeply aware of this utter transcendence of God will be able to interpret to modern atheists their own experience of existence with some hope of success. But they ought not to treat the doctrine of the incomprehensibility of God like an object once possessed but long forgotten in a cup-board, which is now unearthed and dusted for this particular purpose of talking with, say, Jaspers or Buber or Heidegger. Modern man has had the frightful misfortune that God in nature has died for him. Where religion once flowered like a blooming meadow, there is nothing left now but dry clay. Perhaps it is better so; perhaps that religion was like the Pontine Marshes that had to be drained. Nevertheless, the effect remains crushing. The Christian is not allowed to avoid this experience. He shares it as a human being; it may even apply to those presentations of his own religion that were themselves an impoverished cosmological form of the truth of Jesus Christ. The resurrection from this tomb is not brought about by reforms of the Church, but by a change in the mentality of the individual, returning to the origins of his religion. The Church as a whole remembers this every year at the stripping of the altars on Good Friday. Jesus was no enthusiast of creation; he approached his goal, steadfastly setting his face (Luke 9. 51); this was his hour, the sacrifice of his life in the darkness of the Cross. Even all the St Peter's Basilicas and Vatican Museums can do nothing else but glorify the memory of this hour.

This is not to say that the natural experience of contemporary humanity must from the start be interpreted in view of the Passion. This will be one of the concluding aspects, but by no means the only one. Before any Christological interpretation of the time, God's majesty must stand out as the unchangeable background on which the diverse mysteries of Christ are outlined. This must not be a strange God, but one who appears even freer to us, and who, in his freedom, may not only be farther from, but also nearer to us. For he is free to pour out the overwhelming riches of his love. The meaning of our time is that God should be exalted higher above contemporary man who himself occupies a higher position than before, and that man thus exalted should in his turn fall down more humbly before this infinitely exalted Lord. Christians must be more intensely on fire with the love of God; they will have to be so if possible more absolutely, more silently, with less dramatic gestures and forms of devotion, which might still be tolerated in the Baroque period, but became impossible in the nineteenth century. They will have to efface themselves, disappearing in the uniform mass, and by doing so gain in sincerity and intensely humble objectivity. Some at least should be able to do this. Only if this absolute experience has once more become the constant background will it also be differentiated for us in a meaningful economy, taking on the various aspects of the spiritual poverty of the Crib, the hidden years of work, the hurried nomad life of the public activities, and the dread and night of the Cross.

All this and much else can become the inner form of the Christian experience of our time. Joy will not be lacking; nevertheless, the essential joy will be the background of the Resurrection from which all the forms of stripping and detachment are dispensed as gifts of the Holy Ghost which the Son sends from the Father. Everything depends on this poverty towards God and in God, poverty of God in us, as the unknown follower of Tauler described it so impressively in his book on the divine poverty. Then it rests with God whether this "poverty in spirit" is to be experienced as felt or as unfelt "bliss", whether man feels himself incredibly enriched by God's infinity or robbed of all finite things without being aware of having gained God. The quality of God's divinity transcending everything in the world cannot be determined by "nearness" or "distance". The nearness of God who is nearer to man than man is to himself is as overwhelming as his distance, which cannot be bridged, and the aspect of consuming loneliness, which Mechthild and Eckhart called the desert of God.

All those who throughout the epochs of Christian history have had to revitalize the Gospel, came from this background, which gave to the biblical episodes their strangely consuming and burning quality; everything in the Old as well as in the New Testament is flame and tempest, the gentle things even more than the rest. It is quite incomprehensible how a sceptical biblical science could miss this fundamental theme, and thus be mistaken in its judgments from the very start. Surely men, even believers, could never invent such a background, which is diametrically opposed to all the laws of human religious imagination. It is a pity that both orthodox Protestant and Catholic biblical scholars often speak as if the human, historical and philological content of Scripture formed a closed world, and that the divine or "spiritual sense" begins only beyond it. The saints realized how the infinite shines directly through the fearful intensity of the prophets, of Jesus, of Paul and of John; how the human word and gesture are but a thin film before it, while through the mask of the human face those burning eyes are flashing which the apocalyptic seer beheld in bodily vision. How clearly could Augustine, Francis, Ignatius see the Father in the Son! "Smelling and tasting the infinite perfume and the infinite sweetness of the Godhead."

While regretting the absence of great figures in our time, we must not forget the army of those nameless ones who suffer in silence, who have offered, and are still offering, a burnt sacrifice that is generally overlooked, in war and deportation, in camps and torture, victims of the totalitarian powers, externally undistinguished from their unbelieving or weakly believing brethren. From prayers without number, spoken more with the life than with the lips, a figure may yet arise, if God wills it, which will unmistakably point to him. But does this potential of suffering become evident in the forms of contemporary Christendom, in which unbelievers in their distress could read the credible witness of the ever greater God? Has the present moment been grasped and understood, which is always the same for believers and unbelievers? For, if its meaning be veiled to unbelievers, it ought to be understood and made known to the uncomprehending world by Christians. If it is true that God is growing in souls, surely he ought first of all to grow in Christians. When man, having emerged from the world-nature, looks round bewildered in the colder, more lonely space that he forms, indeed that he is, the dignity of his loneliness ought to be interpreted to this puzzled, seemingly forlorn creature. For the most lonely, unique God can only be met in a loneliness worthy of him, communicated from his very Being, the Alone to the alone. This means that the individual of the species leaves the calyx of nature in order to be the individual man before the unique God, whether in solitary private prayer or in the public worship of the assembled Church. But with this we have already reached the next aspect, which needs separate treatment.

B. WORD AND SUPER-WORD

1. *Solitary man and nameless Godhead*

MEN HAVE always regarded solitude as a value; the great world religions share this view with Christianity. They place at the summit of mankind not the social being, but the man who has "emigrated" to God. Once a year the highest priest meets the descending God on the highest terrace of the Babylonian temples. Chinese art centres round the figure of the sage devoted to contemplation in the solitude of rock and waterfall. From the noise and bustle of Western civilization thinkers look longingly towards the gesture of the great Easterners who have left the world. Thus Nietzsche's Zarathustra goes into the mountains into the seventh solitude, the Emperor of China in Claudel's great play *The Repose of the Seventh Day*, having pacified his realm by his descent into hell, departs into the inaccessible mountain temples to look on God alone. Again, at the end of Ludwig Derleth's *Fränkischer Koran*, the grandiose symphony of joy and pain is transfigured and dissolved into the wisdom of the sacredly sober mystical heights of a solitude resembling Mount Athos, and at the end of Gustav Mahler's *Song of the Earth* the "leave-taking" becomes overwhelming and will never end, because it is the last gesture uniting the friends.

The Egyptian Plotinus is an Easterner too, and all the great men of the West, in writing of the value of solitude, looked towards him: the Alexandrines, Ambrose and Augustine, Thomas, Eckhart and Nicholas of Cusa. Independently of him, however, St Anthony followed the call of the desert; and innumerable men followed the saint, to be alone with God through him and in his company. The seekers after solitude are received by the hot rock caves of Athos and, at the other end of Europe, by the cold, barren isles round Ireland and Northern Scotland, unforgettably described by Reinhold Schneider in his *Inselreich* ("Island Kingdom"). The eyes of those left behind will always follow them, irresistibly attracted. No one is less forgotten than the hermit. It seems as if no man could appeal to the hearts of his fellows more effectively than by leaving them and going to God. Therefore the founders of religious orders come from solitude; in caves and walled hiding places they are found after years by a wandering hunter and brought before kings, radiating a solitude that they can never again lose.

The Dominicans, St Thomas Aquinas especially, develop this into a universally valid law: to act from the abundance of contemplation. Solitary contemplation is not only a preparation preceding later action in time, it is the permanent source, resting in itself, from whose abundance the activity in the world is nourished. And though the mixed, active-contemplative life becomes increasingly the characteristic Christian form established by the Mendicant Orders, yet the tradition is so powerful that St Thomas[1] places the eremitical life on an even higher plane: "The common life is necessary for the practice of perfection; but solitude is the part of those who are perfect. Hence the solitary life, if it be undertaken according to the proper order, is above the social life." The ideal of the hermit of Manresa will not change this, let alone that of the great Teresa and of the strange *conquistador* of the transcendent far-eastern islands of God, as St John of the Cross understood himself. Undisturbed by world revolutions, this current flows from Bruno the Carthusian to Rancé the Trappist, and right into the midst of our contemporary world to Charles de Foucauld, who fled from the most austere monasteries into the even barer desert.

Nevertheless, in recent times the form of external solitude has at least been relativized. The solitude of the cosmological age found a last echo in the romantic cult of nature affected by the men and women of the Enlightenment. Tired of civilization, they indulged in Trianons and Peter's Islands, and sang the praises of the solitary life (Zimmermann and Obereit). They produced hermits and "Journals for Hermits", whose place was taken in the nineteenth century by the *Europamüden* (the weary of Europe), and finally by the explorers and heroes who devoted themselves to the service of mankind. Yet all this, too, is already a thing of the past. The external desert has vanished, the white spots on the map have been filled in; the ends of the earth which once merged into the infinite, luring men into uncertain distances, have come near and lost their mystery. The globe, inhabited everywhere, resembles as a whole a one-room flat in which the whole family lives, eats and sleeps, begets children, is sick and dies, in a community that admits of no escape. Socialized man suffers from spiritual asthma and fits of suffocation. The more he numbs his interior void with the drugs of civilization, the more incapable he

[1] II-IIae, q. 188, a. 8.

becomes of loving his neighbour who has come so close to him. Nature, into which he once could escape, has been defaced by science and industry; whatever he may still snatch of it on a Sunday is spoiled by the seething masses and the means of transport. But in himself, too, he no longer finds the landscape in which the solitary man once found his way to the solitary God. Here, too, he lacks breathing space. In his enforced solitude which he is unable to master he can only become a neurotic. And psychiatry, the therapy that has developed together with the disease, is unable to help effectively, for how could it show man the way to God?

The solitary man of today differs from the hermits in that he is the man of the anthropological age. He has been lifted out of nature and can no longer understand himself in the mirror of the macrocosm, hence he is alone with himself as with a stranger. All he knows with certainty of this unknown person is that he is alone, that it belongs to his essence to be alone. Hence it is unpardonably superficial if psychologists simply refer the subject of this experience back into the community. The people he meets there are the same as himself; it is always the same lonely questioner who helplessly turns to the other for advice in his predicament. The lonely man of today meets in the "thou" only himself; he is more narcissistic than ever before in the history of mankind. Two lonely people find in one another always their own inalienable loneliness. At first Eros hides this truth; the normal way of love is to be recalled from surrender to Eros into the essential loneliness. So it is always in Strindberg, Dehmel and Wedekind, also in Hamsun and, above all and as a consciously planned programme, in Sartre.

Thus it is inevitable that today psychiatry and philosophy should meet everywhere. As a science psychology has no other possibility than to explore the natural (*es-haften*—belonging to the Id) elements of the structure of the soul and to attempt to cure the sick soul from there. Yet by doing so it only becomes the counterpart of the disease, that is of the loneliness of the Ego, due to the fact that its natural presuppositions have been made into an object of science. The psychiatrist descends into the "basement" of the soul, bringing to light the foundations of the house in which it dwells, hence the truth he can show has the character of stripping and disclosure, of that disillusion produced by "modern objectivity" that lies at the basis of the world-fear (*Weltangst*) of the modern neurotic. The truth which he is asked to face is itself disastrous like the Medusa; no wonder that he tries to escape it and that it can only "heal" him by destroying even his fear of it. Philosophy as anthropology would necessarily have to start from here (and it does not matter at all that today Heidegger denies his anthropological interest and even makes it the scapegoat of the whole history of philosophy). It would have to characterize the human situation as such, which truly shows itself only in modern man, as this horror (*Entsetzen*) of the spirit emerging from nature when it realizes that it is linked to nature. For nature is that which is below him, which he rules, and which hence is foreign to him. To be thus within foreign surroundings is incredibly sad and frightening. As long as God remains excluded from this anthropology, it cannot solve the human question through the meeting and love between men.

Nevertheless, the modern solitary attempts it by trying to develop this solitude beyond love into an ultimate attitude worthy of man, indeed the only one that will fully reveal his dignity. He is in search of some kind of super-love which, because it is essentially solitude, cannot be expressed directly but is only "mystically" accessible. This modern mysticism with its strong dash of stoicism can be met everywhere. Its relentless character—one might even be tempted to call it its romanticism of matter-of-factness and disillusion—attracts not only the desperate citizens of overpopulated towns, but even Christians. One symptom of it is the fascination the Sahara has exercised on Paris: Rimbaud escapes into it, the hero of Smara, Psichari, and, in his own way, Lyautey; Claudel's Don Camillo, who has his "idea" of Mogador, creates a veritable myth of it. Saint-Exupéry and T. E. Lawrence round off the type, Malraux and his disciples are akin to it. The desert man is the modern "noble man"; he has the qualities of the soldier but without militarism, he is a Stoic but with heroism, hard but without the passion of hardness that Nietzsche ascribed to the "blond beast". His solitude is uncramped and not *exalté*, it is meant to prove that even in the machine age the perfect gentleman still exists, educated precisely by his handling of material to a justice combined with justness, such as had become unknown in the decaying bourgeoisie. Lawrence is the contemplative in politics, Saint-Exupéry in aviation. They are intent on refuting the Christian thesis that in such rarefied atmosphere man can no longer survive. Though their solitude was devoid of God, they yet did not break down; indeed, they would instruct Christians in keeping a perfect balance, in making sacrifices in silence and in the self-oblivion that no longer needs to appeal every moment to the "Cross" in order to stand up to the reverses of fortune. "What matters is to dress, to board the 'plane, to take off. What one thinks oneself is quite irrelevant." Hardness is sought not for its own sake but to survive. "He did not mean to enslave them by this hardness, but to take them out of themselves." The pilot becomes the symbol of transcending nature spiritually. "Seen from these heights, earth seems naked and dead." "World in a display cabinet, all too exposed, too much spread out, too well-ordered on the open map . . . but he is thinking: I am alone." He is alone just as much as the dumb earth beneath him or the endless ocean; he is in the azure above the milky sea of the clouds, or crashed on the tableland in the desert without hope of help, only sun, sand, and the broken wings of his machine. The height and coldness of the flight leave the present world behind as if "buried in the past", "imprisoned in ice". Words as they are spoken among human beings lose their weight. "Even the words most pregnant with meaning like 'tenderness' and 'love' left no ballast in our hearts." The pilot is a monk. Women are left behind, out of sight; yet the external distance is but a faint reflexion of the inner remoteness that is established without force, without moral struggle and resignation, only because solitude has spread its silent, silken, powerful wings around the man it has carried off.

Politics, too, are altogether left behind. The ideal of the "chief" which Saint-Exupéry traces in *Citadelle* may be compared with certain strange historical models as also much in the works of Nietzsche, Spengler or Jünger; yet something different is meant by it. We would nevertheless leave it open whether this noble man, so exalted above all that is low, so gentle in his hardness, so unapproachable yet inspiring devoted service, can possibly exist without a social framework and the weight of a substantial world order, capable of walking through closed doors. Yet thus he is meant to be, not substantial, but, quite in keeping with the technical age, functional. As a machine must be extremely pure and correct to fulfil its function, so must he. Hence he is political neither on the right nor on the left; the question of social justice is for him a problem wrongly posed. Compassion with the small miseries and injustices of the earth spoils the substance of human nature. To try to correct them by bettering the conditions of life means evading the truth of being man. Integrity exists in the solitude either of rightly commanding or of rightly obeying. The man who commands is lonely, because he cannot share his responsibility and can on no account seek human support from his subordinates. He may not even reveal to them his hidden warmth and affection through the crystal cold objectivity of his order. The man who obeys is lonely, too, since he is torn away from his standards of understanding and fellowship, positing an act that isolates him, as he hangs on the vertically falling voice of the command without lateral security. Therefore this solitude is also beyond love, and expressly beyond that absolute relation to God that is interpreted as love. The hero walks out of Notre Dame after a sermon on the love of God that leaves him utterly cold, bad-tempered and disgusted: "I did not hear the act of faith but a perfectly desperate cry. To love, only to love—what an impasse! Rivière had the dark feeling that there is a duty greater than that of loving."

This quotation is representative of the attitude of many others, for example Gide's *L'enfant prodigue*, so attractive to Rilke, who transposed him into his own key in *Malte Laurids Brigge*. It recalls the rejection of "transitive" love in favour of a no longer definable "parallel ray of the heart". The poet has perhaps never been so completely faithful to any other concept as to this, which he almost elevated into his personal dogma. In his interpretation of the *Duineser Elegien* Guardini definitely rejected it; yet ought he not to have given a little more attention to it and to this whole tendency among the moderns? For it is Guardini who calls our attention more imperiously than any other modern Christian thinker to the fact that God is not "the Other", that he is not limited by being opposite. It is salutary for the man who meets God to be conscious of his own limits, of the fact that he is not God. This happens when he listens to the divine Word, in which everything remains a mystery except this one fact that I am not the Word. But what happens if the Word itself wants to be experienced as unlimited, both in its contents and in its form?

Modern man in his solitude seeks passionately as every other generation for the absolute. But he will not let himself be caught either by absolute denominational claims or by idealistic and cosmological enthusiasms. He will not go one step beyond what he can justify with his existence, to what he can pledge himself entirely. Hence his silence. And his silence is neither wise nor exalted nor mystical nor enjoined by responsibilities; it is rather cautious and discreet, springing from the probity of a man who will not say a word for which he is not prepared to risk his life.

The great Christian statements such as "God is love", "God is Trinitarian life", "God is the Word", "God has saved us", "God has become Man and has died on the Cross for us" are lying about in every street. Everybody can touch them with his foot and kick them into the nearest gutter. Surely it is better to avoid them and perhaps to seek that place in existence, in one's heart, where such great statements, or even a smaller one provided it is genuine, can fully be realized. "Where, oh where is the place where the weights are still heavy?" These big notions are both too little and too much. They are too little because they offer too much; they offer things which one may not accept with impunity unless one is willing to pay for them with one's life.

And must we really keep on using this word "love" which has gradually become unbearable, and continue to tear it to rags? Indeed, it is not right that I should call that which makes me solitary beyond all human dialogue by the same name as that which unites me to men. Surely, it is much better that what calls me away from all that can be named on earth should itself remain without a name. It is whole as long as it is nameless. It is the infinite space in which I can bear to live as long as no finite word has invaded it. The ancients said that man is the being who wants to see God. Is this really true? Is there not a sphere in man where he simply does *not* want to see God? This is not the fear of the creature that is afraid of being shattered by him, nor the trembling of the sinner, nor even indifference. It is something that, in the narrow conditions of earth, is called love, but here, on the mountains of the seventh solitude, has cast off this name, by reason of a modesty that neither can nor wants to explain itself. It is due to a need for purity, for preserving one's own and also that of the absolute, and to the horror of the dialectical mess the Idealists have made of things.

All this is being considered by modern man in the world and in his responsibility for it. His solitude is shifted towards the interior, where it is more effectively protected than in the old hermitages, ever since man has become a stranger to himself. From this attitude of being a stranger he opens his heart to those who need him, which is thus only enlarged. From this matter-of-fact attitude for which even the name of humility is too high-sounding, he returns to the love that is always not matter-of-fact (*unsachlich*). He need not even change in this return, he remains the functional type that he was before.

This man indisputably exists. He himself would not assert that he is the solution of the question that is open in man. He would only live with this question in his existence in a not too inadequate, more or less decent, manner. Without meaning to proselytize, he would only tactfully indicate that one can manage in this way, and that it is more advantageous to be silent than to sing difficult metaphysical or theological arias without having the voice for them, as did the pantheists and the cosmic thinkers of the last century.

2. *Intensity*

Before the Christian undertakes to "manage" this solitary contemporary, to improve or even to convert him, he ought first to ask himself how he intends to meet him. And, as before, he will ask himself whether this man is perhaps experiencing something that might also be suitable for himself, who is so well versed in love and community; indeed, something that may have been meant for him even more particularly. This is an experience which he has quite inexplicably lost.

If we ask ourselves which movements within the Church have received a certain response during the last three decades, if not among the crowd, which rarely has much enthusiasm for movements, at least among the intellectuals, three are outstanding: the Biblical Movement, the Liturgical Movement, and the Personalist Movement. The first two may be said to be efforts within the Church to make up for things that have long been neglected by going back to the sources. The third, connected with Scheler, was the organic reaction to, and the complement of, Neo-Scholasticism. A fourth is beginning to be outlined as a movement of the laity in the Church and of a corresponding "theology of the earthly realities".[1] Here, too, lost truths are being retrieved and adapted. It is evident, however, that the Christian who perhaps joins his silent brother in his lonely walk can hardly introduce himself as the envoy or herald of a "movement". In fact, the idea is not to involve him in a discussion or to make the silent man talk. The question is rather whether the Christian is a match for this silence.

He could be if he had experienced the abyss of silence from which springs the Word of God, and also in its wake and in response to it, the essential human word, whose mystery the former holds, unveils and makes visible before it returns whence it came. This is an experience of faith breathing the air of infinity from the bosom of the Father which can never be adapted to the earthly level. All the words—those that have been said and those left unsaid—all the gestures and deeds of Jesus Christ are not only surrounded by silence, they are steeped in the ineffable, drawn from silence, and can be detached from their invisible background against which the figure stands and by which it is supported on all sides, so that it would lose all meaning and reality apart from it. The Biblical Movement, too, can only have a meaning if we seek and sense in the Word that which is beyond the world, that Word which expresses itself by all individual words, and, indeed, not itself, but the Father who is silent in It. Again, liturgy means association with its silent Sacraments which are the background of the Church's formal language in prayers and sermons. And Personalism rightly understood leads man to adore him who is

[1] Roger Aubert, *La théologie catholique au milieu du 20e siècle*, Casterman, 1954.

higher than all we call ego and person in the world. Jesus prayed to the Father in words when he stood before his disciples or wanted to teach them words of prayer. But who shall say whether and in how far he used words when he poured out his soul above himself (as St Augustine says of the man in prayer) into the infinity of the Father? Who can even stammer of what it means to him to see the Father; the fathomless origin not only of the world, but of God himself; him who reveals himself to us in the Son and is visible in him, and again in the Holy Ghost transcending all form? For the Spirit is at the same time what appears and what does not appear of God, he who makes the Father visible for us in the Son, and who for this very reason lets the limits of the appearance of the Son again become transparent in the infinity of the Father. "That while we know God visibly we may be rapt through him into the love of invisible things." Surely the Fathers were right to reject the idea that the vision of God promised to the perfect man would reveal his whole mystery—whereas it is rather the open vision of the abyss of his mystery without which he would not be God. *Si comprehendis, non est Deus*: this must also hold good for the "comprehensor". God is the *mysterium fascinosum*, not only relatively and during our time on earth; but absolutely and for ever. Having supremely revealed the character of his mystery as grace in the abandonment of his Son during the time of our mortality, he will reveal it to be our bliss in eternity.

For thus it is fitting. He must always be the greater, above and beyond all . . . not only in this, but also in the future world, so that God may always remain the teacher, and that man as the disciple may always learn from God. For the Apostle, too, says that when all else shall have vanished, these three alone will remain: faith, hope and charity. For our faith in our Teacher will always remain unshaken, giving us the certainty that he alone is the true God, that we love him for ever, because he is the unique Father, and thus we may also hope to receive something more from God and to learn from him, because he is the Good One, possessing inexhaustible riches and a Kingdom without end.[1]

[1] Irenaeus, *Contra Haereses*, 2.28.3.

These are the words of that Father of the Church who fought most violently against the Gnostic heresy and mocked bitterly their invention of empty silence, of a hollow abyss in God, and who yet affirmed that Christians know that the mystery cannot be dissolved. A word of revelation, even a word of any fellow man, that would have ceased to be steeped in mystery would have ceased at the same time to be a word worth listening to. It is an echo of the divine depth that belongs to the "image and likeness" of the divine Being in the creature, that nothing that is, that shares in the mystery of Being, is completely defined by its appearance; and it would betray an inferior idea of *ratio* to suspect this fundamental law or irrationalism. When Christians, too, once more become aware of this law, they will learn to realize that God is no "object", not even of knowledge, but that he remains "ineffably superior" even to the category of objectivity.[1] Hence in the category of the "other", the "thou", too, he can only be included analogically.

Here the mystery of the analogy of personality once more raises its head; yet it is only the mystery of the analogy of being applied to the spiritual creature. We are persons so dependent on what we cannot call other than the personality of God, that the more we are persons the more fully we also share in his freedom. So we become the more independent, the more intensely we serve him; the freer, the more we share in his divine Law; the more unified and simple, the more we participate in his unique oneness and solitude. This is an inevitably dialectical formulation; but its necessity is self-evident, though it can never be fully elucidated, despite all the efforts of metaphysics and Christian revelation to throw light on it. It casts a strange light on what human solitude *can* be, indeed on what it *must* be, if it is to be an answering image of the divine solitude.

Human solitude has the possibilities of being either completely closed or completely open to God. But human recollection and silence have no possibility of being neutral to God. Hence they are in any case dialogical, whether they want to or not. They can only face God or turn their back on him. Everyone knows how two people who hate each other can be engaged in the most

[1]Denzinger, 1782.

violent and exhausting dialogue while silently turning their backs
to each other, expressing as much by the gesture of turning away
as others by facing each other. Here, however, we do not speak
of the man who hates God, of Cain, the sinner who flees from
God, yet everywhere bears conspicuously the sign of God on
his forehead, but of the solitary man who is near him. This man
knows, and yet does not know, the ineffable mystery that, being
a truly solitary man, *he rests in solitude*. And in this silence takes
place the only really decisive thing that can happen: he is open,
he abandons the frontier, he raises the barrier in order to let pass
—as wordlessly as he himself—whatever wants to cross his
frontier. Buber once described it as something that happens
between two people who are silent together: "The solution has
happened to him without his own contribution, wherever it
may have come from. But now what he does is to release what
held him back, over which he alone has power. Without restraint
the communication flows out from him, the silence carries it to
his neighbour. . . . What does he now 'know' of the other? He
needs no longer any knowledge. For where restraint has ceased
between men, even though it may have happened without words,
there the dialogical word has sacramentally taken place." And
then, applied to God: "He who practises the real dialogical
responsibility need not name the speaker of the word to whom
he replies—he knows him in the substance of the word that moves
him in his heart of hearts, insistent, invading, taking on the accents
of interiority. A man may reject the existence of God, and yet
savour him in the austere sacrament of the dialogue."[1]

If Buber as a Jew here uses the word Sacrament metaphorically,
a Christian should see from this how much the Christian Sacrament is a super or substantial word, and how much therefore
the all-sacramental structure of the Christian revelation or
"economy" bears this character as a whole. The Sacrament
(*sacramentum, mysterion*) bears without words, even though
mediated by the word of the Church, the depth of the divine
mystery into the soul of the creature and silently opens it to this
silent depth. Even the word of the Church in which the Sacrament
is embedded can only adoringly circle round this depth in its

[1]*Zwiesprache*, 1947, 135; 155.

centre. Even a word of personal thanksgiving can do no more for this unknown, unfathomable gift. Nothing can be expressed in words; if a man speaks he can never acquit himself. If his words signify that he is open, they will have the secret mark of truth for those who are susceptible to it, of falsehood, if they hide the fact that he is closed to God. But we are not simply concerned to place the word at a deeper level, from the spoken audible to the silent inaudible exchange. What matters is that in this depth of communion, which does not for a moment overlook the analogy between God and the creature, but rather is an aspect of it, the "objectivity" (*Gegenständigkeit*) reveals itself as "intensity" (*Inständigkeit*).

This realm of solitude has yet another dimension (*Spanne*): that extends from "nature" to "supernature". As "nature" it has its form in that mysticism which, following a genuine law of obedience (though here there is also much disobedience), turns away from all objects. It knows that there is a danger of straying into a void, but also a chance of approaching the place where finite things spring from the infinite, catching a breath, as it were, of the origin that lies, beyond all creature, in God. As "supernature" solitude has the form of the indwelling of the Holy Spirit in the inmost sphere of the creature's ego, so that all its thoughts and desires are nourished from the deeper divine source, and the ego as a whole has become receptive for the streams of divine life passing through it. And this supernatural solitude shows yet another extension. That between the hidden mystery of grace working as it were *ex opere operato* in every Christian soul, and the flowering of this mystery into the central law of the whole personal life, such as Thomas Aquinas describes it as the development of the gifts of the Holy Ghost. One cannot, however, depict this experienced indwelling of the Spirit of God as an awareness of being indwelt; this is impossible because the infinite God cannot dwell in the finite ego as in an habitation containing him. It can only be experienced as a widening of the finite person which is born into an infinite one, as if his limited house was becoming transparent. This happens not only in such a way that the walls would be turned into glass, and scenery and stars included in the world of its inhabitant, but so that the glass is replaced by a living wave which, itself transparent, streams through the transparent element. If in the man who does not know how to pray (perhaps because God is too great, too far, or too near) the Spirit calls out, "Abba, Father", this word, which is not audible but perhaps only a silent word of being, sounds from a place that can be said to be neither in nor outside the soul. "He is nearer to me than I am myself."

This is the stage where St Thérèse of Lisieux no longer desired to see God, but lowered her eyes because she was so close to him. *Baisser les yeux*, not because the power of vision is, as it were, overstrained, but because vision *wants* to pass into non-vision, into letting-be, into pure adoration without any definite affirmation. There are not only many things we do not tell God because they are too secret or so as not to burden him with them, as it were; for we would not give an importance to our own concerns which, on the contrary, we ardently want to take away from them. Above all we are silent, in order to give room to his silence, we do not look at him so as not to be noticed, not to attract his attention to ourselves, not to play the rôle of the some-how equal partner, but to let God be all in all. The mystery of the lowered eyes was revealed on the Cross, when the Father was silent when the Son called on him, and the dying Son inclined his head so as no longer to see heaven but the earth. It was shown again in the descent into hell, when, on Holy Saturday, Nietzsche is right for just one day and God is dead. The Word has ceased to sound in the world, the body is buried and sealed, and the soul descends into the abyss of Sheol, where death rules in all reality and is not defeated beforehand by faith, love and hope, where the *poena damni* includes all, that is the impossibility of seeing God, looking for him, raising the eyes to him. (And even if, in a complementary conception, the light of hope is thought to exist even before Christ, this is still due to Christ, to his incipient coming.) Here the love between Father and Son has adopted the mode of estrangement, of nearness abolished, of incomprehensibility, in order to include in itself all men's estrange-ment through sin. How should there not be an imitation of Christ also in this? The disciples cry out when they see Jesus walk upon the water at night: he seems a ghost to them. He knows it, but does nothing to avoid this impression. God—as a ghost; love—exciting horror. The approaching nearness—that which causes senseless flight. But if the eternal Being could not also appear to us as a void in order to show Its true superiority to us (as the void of all that we are and that the world is)—how could it be the eternal Being?

The mystery of the "always greater dissimilarity" of God, however great may be the similarity between him and the creature, has attracted only few thinkers. Erich Przywara is one of them; all his thought and poetry bear witness to it. His verse as well as his thought move everywhere close to the border where the word passes into silence, where finite passes into infinite movement, and thus, from the earthly point of view, ceases altogether. Dom Vandeur's prayers carry this knowledge into the ranks of the contemplatives of the Church. Max Picard's *World of Silence* points to it in most impressive words. Reinhold Schneider represents the man who, coming from there, does his daily work in the Church and the world; and this man walks beside such as Saint-Exupéry, Malraux and T. E. Lawrence.

"To lower the eyes" (instead of striving after "sight" and the "idea" as if they were the highest goals) means to choose obedience and put it in the place of understanding. Certainly this does not mean a "blind" obedience that gives up thought, nor an obedience intent on seeing. The obedience meant by it corresponds to, and springs from, that in-tensity which at its highest means that man is moved by the Holy Ghost. This is the idea of ecclesiastical obedience: of the Body-Church moved by its Head and of the member that obeys with it wherever the Church obeys its Lord. It is a place of absolute solitude, of ecstasy above all that is understood, and hence connects and creates relations, the place of the Son's ecstasy on the Cross into the pure, no longer comprehended, will of the Father; of the Mother of the Lord into the pure *Fiat* without limits; of every creature that penetrates into the truth of "Thy will be done". The highest acts of the Church are accomplished in loneliest responsibility, and this is identical with obedience. It is the merit of Reinhold Schneider to have shown up this act as the source of all sacred and secular history. His kings and his saints standing opposite each other are united in the same silence and obedience. Philip II, flanked by St Teresa and St Ignatius, represents all others. He can look at the "Chief" of Saint-Exupéry without blinking. It does not matter to him whether or not he is understood by his subjects. He embodies order, because he himself obeys. The most incredible citadel of Christendom, the monastery-palace of the Escorial, is the silent order of the stars turned into stone within a desert landscape, and the silent king who inhabits it is its heart that has become a star. Schneider knows, indeed, that the Escorial is Baroque and belongs to the past, to an order of representation that can no more be restored. Yet the present and the future of Christendom depend on this, whether an Escorial of silent obedience rises again in individuals. The action in a wider sphere as represented by the Church's call to the laity will avoid being frittered away in irrelevancies only if the interior spires of invisible cathedrals rise always equally high into the mystery of God. The Marienburg once stood on the border of the Eastern steppe as a German Escorial; the spiritual obedience of those who dwelt in it was older than its secular Prussian type. It was the hidden form which nourished all visible cultural achievements. It remains the secret treasure of the Church. For the Son has not redeemed the world by humanitarian and social works, but by the blood of his obedience shed in apparent frustration on the Cross, by which he penetrated beyond the sphere of the social as well as of the personal factors into the nameless and faceless silence of the God-head which, being three-personal, transcends the personal.

C. Being Lost

1. *The rebels and the hells*

TODAY people are afraid to use the concept of hell seriously, because it has recently been so much abused by literary people as to become quite hackneyed. There are now not only the hells of Stalingrad and Hiroshima, there are also the spiritual and intellectual hells which are brought on to the stage by Sartre and set to music by Adrian Lewerkühn. Consequently, it is understandable that the Church and its theologians are using this conception more sparingly than ever; indeed, there is actually a kind of hesitation to speak about it at all. The last serious book on the subject is certainly more than half a century old.

We would take up this theme here only in the literary (*geisteswissenschaftlich*) context. We consider the fashionable interest in hell to be a symptom of a spiritual situation which cannot be overlooked, because it is so universal and constant in its expression. We shall then ask whether there is an actual or possible Christian reply to this question of our time.

The change from cosmology to anthropology already described contains all that is needed to explain this phenomenon. Man who has emerged from the protective framework of nature into unprotected freedom can only experience his new position in— and partly above—the cosmos in two directions. On the one hand, it is the freedom to contradict the divinely appointed cosmic order in a fundamental and highly effective sense, and thus also to defy the God of the cosmos and the Christian God of love who has so far been identified with him. The experience of man's loneliness in this world, which can no longer be his partner because it obeys him, is here deepened to the experience of the loneliness of the man given over to evil, who experiments with the possibilities of freedom, who "enacts" his existential distance from God by systematically investigating its dimensions. Thus the old pagan and Christian imagery of Hades and hell was inevitably not only found suitable, but actually indispensable.

So the devil has become a familiar figure ever since Ivan Karamazov talked to him over the table, while Lewerkühn repeated the same conversation, and Abbé Donissan was led in circles by him throughout the night, wrestling with him breast to breast. Rimbaud, in his turn, spent *une saison en enfer*, inducing all the poets to try to follow in his footsteps; Sigmund Freud conducted his investigations of psychological depths under the motto *Acheronta movebo*, thus giving scientific standing to the experience of Schiller's *Diver*: "Down there it is horrible". The characters of Strindberg, Wedekind and Sartre have offered instructive examples of the hell of love, marriage and social existence in general: "hell is the others".

The Christian ideas of hell had received their first shock as early as the Baroque period. The Middle Ages had seen it as the seriously objective and adequate Christian threat to the individual and to the multitude, and therefore depicted it over the doors of its cathedrals. But in Abraham a Santa Clara's *Arch Knave* and in Scheffler's *Last Things* it had already been given a forced theatrical note. The old Hades, shedding its Christian costume of hell, begins to be an indispensable operatic requisite, at first playfully ambivalent, as it still is in Gluck's *Orpheus*. But the truly abysmal Baroque pathos of transitoriness and forlornness does not yet untilize this theme. Milton seems to be the turning point: this blind, embittered man turns the rebel against God into a hero. His line of thought is not continued in the weakly Satan of Klopstock, but in Lessing's fragment of *Faust*, which was soon to be followed by Goethe's drama. Here the idea was that the spirit that had come of age in the Enlightenment should get to know its true greatness in the attempt at denial. Surely it ought to add the dramatic, interesting dimension of a game of life and death to the flat and boring breadth of its new knowledge by opening the abyss and thus changing the dim light of "enlightenment" into an authentic flame.

The change is imperceptible, and yet suddenly the altogether other makes its frightening appearance as an accomplished fact. There has always been guilt in the world, but it was considered to be that which ought not to be, and so to require atonement. This view is left fundamentally unchanged even if guilt be so inextricably entangled in man's existence that he is tragically thrown into it, as were the heroes of Greek tragedy. But now guilt becomes the condition of being spirit, a moment of nature itself, necessarily posited in order to be as necessarily overcome. Negation as such is creative, says Hegel; existence as such is guilty, says Heidegger. In order to exist, man must effect the negation which gives him both guilt and spirit at the same time.

This idea is an interior revolt first of all against the concept of guilt itself, which is only intelligible if it is something that ought not to be, presupposing a prohibition; but more profoundly against the concept of God, to whom alone the guilt of this must be ascribed, and who must be held responsible for having created a being that becomes guilty because it exists. Here it becomes immediately evident that the two formulas are possible only within a dialectic, since the one assertion must be posited and denied simultaneously in order to make the other possible. Guilt must be what ought not to be (and hence cannot exist necessarily) if it is not to annihilate itself; and this notion alone permits the notion of a God for whom evil is real and hence an abomination which he punishes. As soon as evil is placed within the order of nature, its own idea as well as that of God are abolished.

This dialectic is nothing else but the correct expression of the lack of logic of the rebellion itself, which can affirm itself only in this and in no other way. The uncanny feature of the rebellion is therefore the perfidious way in which it both posits and annihilates God, visualizing him as the true God in order to be able to proclaim him effectively to be a bogey-man. For why should a man enjoy uttering the blasphemy if he had not the secret satisfaction of being heard by him whom he blasphemously declares not to exist? Thus in the course of the nineteenth century and down to our own day there has developed a veritable kind of science of revolt. Its systematic procedure corresponds to what the Apocalypse stigmatizes and forbids under the expression "know the depths of Satan" (2.24), but which becomes intelligible only within a dialectic circling round itself.

A first form of it is still predominantly romantic; it may be summed up in the formula: "I am finding myself guilty, hence I accuse God." Evil is felt as the tragic feature of existence; now the tragic excites pity; hence the most wicked creature, the demon, must rouse an extreme compassion. It is characteristic that sober, positivist England should have been the first to unseal the abyss from which will ascend "the smoke of the pit, as the smoke of a great furnace" (Apoc. 9.2). Even Shakespeare was fascinated by the abyss; and Marlowe, who was a good deal tougher, still more. After Milton comes Blake, who looks deliberately for what is evil and blasphemous, and Byron, who glorifies Cain and demands pity for Lucifer. The French follow suit with the uncanny Sade who is echoed in the Satanic litanies of Baudelaire and certain devilries of Balzac. From then onward there has been no end of a dandyish cult of Satan. In Germany it needed more time for the poison of Faust to penetrate the organism. Only in the middle of the last century did a sour, self-destructive pessimism gain ground, gnawing at the roots of life. Jacob Boehme had prepared for it by naturalizing evil in God as well as in man. Schelling's philosophy of freedom started from there: the possible and actual "No" in the heart of his creatures' freedom is ideally co-eternal with God; hence there is within God himself an eternal, darkly-flaming abyss, a hell within heaven. This is a far more demonic conception than the "creative negation" in Hegel's system, where there is no God worth contradicting. Berdyaev has once more been as intensely frightened of the abyss as Schelling; Marcel Jouhandeau only seconds him when he says: "I can by myself raise up a kingdom against God over which God has no power; that is hell." Thus from the very beginning the knowledge of the devil becomes a form of self-knowledge, perhaps the most profound spiritual and intellectual reflexion. To quote once more Jouhandeau: "If a man does not understand hell this means that he has not understood his own heart." How quickly pandemonism conquered Germany is shown by the unexampled success of Schopenhauer among the half-educated: the ground of the world itself is evil and blind. From this thought that has sprung from deep *ressentiment* we shall then pass on rapidly and smoothly to the unclean myths of Wagner and the even more equivocal ones of Thomas Mann.

But for the moment the revolt still has the character of an indictment of God. He is accused of having created or permitted guilt, of having produced the devil, this most miserable of all creatures, for whom the poets weep and with whom they make common cause. It is the old complaint of Marcion against the Demiurge, given literary form in the poems of the Last Judgment, in which God no longer judges the world, but the indignant universe of creatures sits in judgment upon God who has failed and is rejected for ever. This motif is to be found from Quinet to Spitteler's *Extramundana*.

Here the first formula changes into a second one: "I have been outwitted by being led into guilt. I protest against the guilt that has been forced on me." With this man enters the vicious circles of Ivan Karamazov and the whole hall of mirrors of the endless works of Dostoievsky. Ivan rejects the "entrance ticket" to heaven because he cannot bear the world order, particularly the redemption provided by it, which causes the depth of guilt to be degraded to a Hegelian moment that has been cancelled out. He pillories innocent suffering as "crying to heaven", thus himself becoming a man who cries to heaven for ethical reasons, appealing against the God of love and universal reconciliation to an unknown God of justice beyond. This is speaking dialectically, because there cannot be two Gods, and this dialectic becomes apparent in the "Grand Inquisitor", a piece written by Ivan, where the order of love, that is of real Christianity, proves unbearable for men. Hence the Inquisitor gently falsifies it according to a plan of inner-worldly justice; nevertheless, the falsifier's own consciousness of guilt and the infinite silence of the Accused Jesus remain.

Kafka's whole work is placed within this dialectic; for he keeps on retracing the steps from the external pronouncement of guilt unexpectedly sprung upon man to its acknowledgment by the accused. It is left open, however, whether this acknowledgment springs from inner conviction or is caused by increasing, inescapable pressure from without; that is to say whether human guilt finally exonerates God or, on the contrary, increasingly and fatally incriminates him. *The Penal Colony* is perhaps the most cruel expression of this terrible ambiguity, which repeats in secularized form the Old Testament, Jewish situation of Job. In the Book of Job the suffering plaintiff against God, conscious of no interior fault, is constantly clamouring for an umpire between him and this incomprehensibly cruel God with whom he cannot come to terms; yet he is finally acquitted by God himself, whereas his friends who tell him to give in and to admit his guilt, are finally condemned only for the sake of Job. The just man, the Jew, pleads with God; that is his privilege, which Kafka again claims for himself. But the God with whom he is concerned is so heavily veiled that one no longer knows whether he exists at all. Perhaps he only signifies the direction in which man utters his complaints. In contrast with the God of Job, this God is no longer loved at all.

The dialectic goes further. It leaves to these just men (or are *Les Justes* of Camus precisely for this reason the unjust?) the concern to justify themselves and turns to the unjust. These explore the depths of the "No" without humour, systematically, even pedantically. How many steps are leading downward, where does one reach the lowest abyss of this house the upper stories of which are inhabited by man? Dante had descended step by step, as a pure, unconcerned man among the shades. But why, in order to be more intimately present, should we not become shades ourselves? We must have the courage to approach the darker possibility, the perversion of the good. It is only consistent that sexual perverts now should take over the leadership, and also that they represent perversion as the real, true, and essentially more interesting form of love. Oscar Wilde, Stefan George and André Gide justify the pervert on the highest level; generations of young people have subscribed to this teaching. Thomas Mann enlarges it by seeking out much more spiritual forms of decay (*Verwesung*); here the downward ways become logically ways of deeper spiritualization; a dialectic of life deriving from Schopenhauer, Wagner and Nietzsche forms the philosophical background. According to this view the ascent and increasing refinement of the spirit is always simultaneously the decadence and degeneration of life. This was first stated in *The Buddenbrooks* in a form that still seemed harmless; soon, however, it became visible less harmlessly in *Welsung Blood, Death in Venice* and *The Magic Mountain* in its calculated reversal: the light of the spiritual and the interesting, even of the actually beautiful, is the phosphorescence produced by the decomposition of what is immediately and crudely healthy. If life is a disease of being, spirit is a disease of life; and the higher the spirit, the more diseased will be the life. The fact of being a genius is (in *Doctor Faustus*) dialectically one with *lues*, hence the atrocious hell in which Lewerkühn imprisons himself by his pact with the Devil is again dialectically one with the heaven of his art. The last glacial point of Satan which Mann takes over from Dante and develops into the feeling of existence (*Existenzgefühl*), this point of indifference and of eternal death is represented with inexorably compelling, overwhelming dialectic as the necessary presupposition of all genuine intellectual and spiritual life. Hence in Adrian's last compositions the harmonies represent hell, whereas the dissonances express the heavenly world. This theme is carried through with strict logic, and the incredible sterility of

the perverted mind is represented as the highest form of genius.
It is not our intention to enumerate all the similar, but less able,
productions more or less consciously derived from this central
dialectic. It will suffice to name the fourth and last variation of this
dialectic:

"I not only do what is evil because this contains what is good,
spiritual and more delicate (this was the third form), but I do the
good from a will to evil. I rob God of his good and do it against
him." That coldest point of indifference of spiritual death supposed to be the highest, actual life has already been reached;
Sartre develops it as that point of absolute "freedom" beyond God
and devil and the two kingdoms that belong to them (*Le Diable
et le Bon Dieu*), which is the point of ultimate distance where man
is detached from all natural necessity that shelters and protects
him. In Sartre's *Nausée*, in his nausea and disgust with goodness
and love, is expressed, in an unequivocal though catastrophic
form, the experience of the transcendence of man in the anthropological age. In the cosmological age *natura*, sheltering, guiding
and justifying man, caused him to appear as a nature among other
natures, with the sole difference that he was the rational animal,
endowed with the organism of reason and will tending towards
infinite truth and goodness, that belonged to his reasonableness.
This *natura*, which a St Thomas Aquinas valued so highly, has for
Sartre become the arch-enemy, the prison of freedom. The
decisive act of becoming man (*Menschwerdung*) is to blow it up.
He is nauseated by the idea of running along the predetermined
lines of decisions permitted by a Demiurge, as a dotted line is
filled in or a river flows in the bed dug for it. Because of this
disgust man transcends these lines, creating the distance of indifference, in which at last everything, good as well as evil, is done in
freedom, hence worthy of man. In the programmatic play just
mentioned he proves that, if taken by themselves, both "articula-
tions", that towards the good and that towards evil, must fail
and are meaningless if they are detached from the acting point of
indifference.

However far the existentialist is from the Marxist, one can
quickly change into the other. For the latter, too, is concerned to
dry up, as it were, the river-bed of organic-intellectual *natura*

(by reducing it to mere economic laws), so that the realm of freedom may spring directly from there. But this drying up demands, in the same way as in Sartre, that the string be cut which joins the creature to the Creator and through which it is naturally dependent on, and guided by, him. Thus the good that once seemed a grace from God is now realized by man himself, and if necessary against God. The existentialist is united with the Marxist in one common anthropological front, because both hold that God belongs to the ideology of the cosmological age, and that Christianity together with its Founder is dangerous and hateful nonsense which grudges man the maturity he has now reached, and would defraud him of it.

Nevertheless, this front also crumbles if we consider that the modern Russian secularized eschatology not only inherits the Western, but no less the Eastern Christian eschatology as it has been handed down from the Greek Fathers through Byzantium to the slavophile Sophiologists and Dostoievsky. If hell has been let loose in the West by the revolt of freedom and the protest of the lonely, free ego, it has always been alive in the East in the sense of a protest of the community against the idea that one of its members should be lost. Even the Christian East has hardly been able to accept the doctrine of possible, let alone actual, damnation as a neutral tenet believed to be true. It has ever again abhorred it as something frightful and impossible. Clement and Origen, Gregory of Nazianzus and Gregory of Nyssa, Evagrius, Maximus and many others get round it by a secret certainty of faith that grace will have mercy on all. This Greek hope of universal redemption lives on in the Russians in a new, if possible even more deeply rooted, form: it is founded on the consciousness of the solidarity of all men.

Is there, perhaps, in the Asiatic mind a sense of the limitlessness of divine grace that cannot be found in the precise thought of the West? Or is it a sense of the interchangeability of persons and destinies, because there, too, the frontiers between mine and thine are not established with such a finality as with us? They say not only: what happens to you might also have happened to me: but: what happens to you I feel as if it had happened to me. The "mystical Body" is thoroughly experienced by its members, and if one member suffers, all the others suffer with him. For the Russian this is not one part of Christianity among others, for him it is its centre and its heart. On this feed the *starets* Sossima, Alyusha and Prince Myshkin, but, after all, even the "swine" Svidrigailov in *Crime and Punishment* and Ivan, the rebel. For Ivan becomes a rebel when his children suffer; he does not want heaven if its harmony has to be bought by innocent suffering. In this idea Sossima's religion joins Karl Marx, who refuses to tolerate a bourgeois heaven on earth as long as the proletarian suffers innocently in hell. Rather let all go to hell, so that, in the community of the proletariat in which alone is salvation, all may find heaven on earth together.

Thus East and West are far from each other and yet near: hell is other people, says Sartre, because the lonely ego can feel love only as something unbearable, because it finds in the others only itself in an unendingly mirrored loneliness. Hell is other people, say also Dostoievsky, Leskov, Berdyaev, because love compels them to the last to stake their soul for their lost brethren. But in this way the whole newly arisen question of man's lost state does indeed become somewhat more serious than it seemed in the beginning. Evidently this consideration of hell is no longer concerned to depict eternal suffering imaginatively, as was so often the case in the Middle Ages and again in Hieronymus Bosch and Breughel, though here the curiosity about dread and perversion is already awake in a surprisingly modern sense. Yet neither is it primarily interested in an aesthetic investigation of the demonic world as in Flaubert's *Temptation of St Anthony*; but it is a concern that is at least serious in its questioning and deserves a hearing. The crashes of those four dialectical steps, the will and urge towards hell expressed in them, cause average commonsense to regard the modern preoccupation with hell as a nonsensical perversion. Yet its evident connexion with the spiritual situation of modern man will not allow us to disregard the whole thing as mere humbug. Both things are true: as the naked freedom of man appears, the abyss of being eternally lost is open, as Schelling has shown. And this, as the Russians know and even the Westerners suspect, is an open problem of human solidarity which is perhaps insoluble but cannot simply be rejected. If the Eastern world has been tempted to secularize the Christian question by taking over Western ideologies, the Western world that has remained Christian ought to be prepared to examine and interest itself in the authentic question of the East. Thus could be formulated what may be taken to be the contemporary Christian answer to the question of the lost man, the lost brother.

2. *The journey through Hades*

The revelation of Jesus Christ contains most fully the truth for every age, hence also for our own. But it contains it not as reaching the faithful without their co-operation, their reflecting on this gift of truth. This would be unworthy both of the grace and of the man who receives it. The Holy Spirit reveals to each age that side of the divine truth which has been specially reserved for it, if the age strives for it in prayer. And this truth does not then lie in some out-of-the-way corner that has so far happened to remain unnoticed and is only now lit up by the Spirit. It is always in the centre, in the fiery furnace whence the light radiates, from where Christians have strayed unawares into ease and comfort, and into which they must return.

What follows is something quite simple. In the first chapter we pointed to the transcendent God, in the second to the divine mystery hidden within every word of God. Both were quite simple, elementary truths of Christianity. It is the same with the Redemption of man which has now to be considered. We will not treat it in a technical theological way; a technical presentation would require a very large historical and systematic approach, for which space is lacking. But even if we treated the matter as exhaustively as possible, it would remain no less mysterious in the end than at the beginning. We should only have made more windows allowing us to gaze at the landscape of the mystery. Thus the present treatment remains the fragment of a fragment, but it aims at the centre, which we mean to consider in a very simple way.

The Christian East has preserved a certain tradition of the Redemption which has been lost to the West at an early stage. The Western image of the Redemption is Golgotha: the crucified

Christ between the two thieves (how much is contained in this "between"!), assisted by Mary, the Mother Church, and John, the apostle of love, to whose care she is entrusted. It is the image of the suffering Man (while the Divinity remains invisible) and of the earthly fruit of this suffering. The heavenly fruit remains even more deeply hidden in the symbolism of the thieves. For the East the image of Redemption is the descent of Christ into Hades: the bursting open of the eternally-closed gate, when Christ stretches out his hand to the first Adam who, hardly trusting his eyes, sees the Easter light in the darkness of death. Thus the Greek Fathers have always preached, thus the Byzantines and the Russians have made visible the other-worldly event of the Redemption. We will quote one of them:

What is this? Great silence reigns on earth today, great silence and loneliness, great silence, for the King is asleep, "the earth trembled and was still", for God is asleep in the flesh and has gone to wake up those who have been asleep during the ages. God has died in the flesh, and Hades trembles. God is asleep for a while and has roused from their sleep the dwellers in Hades. He goes to seek Adam, the first-created, and primeval Father, the lost sheep. All those who sit in darkness and the shadow of Death he will go to visit. He goes there to free Adam from his bonds and Eve, fettered with him, from her sorrows—both God and her Son.

So let us descend with him, to see the covenant of God with man. There is Adam, the primeval Father, imprisoned and buried deeper than all the others that are condemned, because he is the first-born. There is Abel, his first-born, who is the first just shepherd and therefore the type of the murder of Christ, the Shepherd. There is Noe, the similitude of Christ, who built the great ark of God which is the Church; there is Abraham, the father of Christ, the sacrificer who offered God the bloody-unbloody, deathly-undeathly sacrifice. There sojourns Moses in the lower darkness, who once sojourned in the upper darkness of the Tabernacle. There sits Daniel in the den of the netherworld, who once sat in the lions' den in the upper world. There is Jeremias in the muddy cave of Hades, in the decay of death. There in the world-embracing monster of Hades sits Jonas, the type of Christ, and one of the prophets cries: "From the belly of Hades give ear to my supplication, hear my voice", and another one: "From the depth I cry to thee, Lord, Lord hear my voice", and yet another: "Let thy countenance shine and we shall be saved."

As now the Lord by his Coming wanted to fetch the lowest of the low, Adam, the primeval Father and first-born of all men, he the first mortal, who is in the interior of all and imprisoned with great care, he was the first to hear the steps of the Lord approaching, when he came to the prisoners. And he knew his voice, as he walked through the prison, and he turned to all who had been chained with him from the beginning of the world and said: "I hear the steps of one coming to us." And while he was speaking, the Lord entered with the victorious standard of the Cross. And when the first Father Adam saw him, he struck his breast in astonishment and called out to the others: "My Lord be with you all". And Jesus answered and said: "And with thy spirit." And he seized his hand and said: "Arise, thou sleeper, arise from the dead, and Christ will illumine thee. I am thy God, and through thee I have become thy son. Arise, thou sleeper, for I have not created thee to lie fettered here in Hades. Arise from the dead, I am the life of the dead. Arise thou my creature, my form, created to my image and likeness. Come and let us go hence, for thou art in me and I in thee, and both of us together are one single and inseparable Person. For thy sake I, thy God, became thy son, and for thy sake I, the Lord, took the form of a slave; for thy sake I, who dwell above all the heavens, descended to earth and under the earth, for thee, Man, I became 'as a helpless man', 'free among the dead', for thee, who left the garden, I was delivered over to the Jews in a garden and crucified in a garden. See on my face the spittle which I received for thy sake, to bring you back to paradise. See on my cheeks the strokes which I bore to restore and transform thy destroyed beauty into my own image. See on my back the strokes of the scourge which I accepted to take from thee the burden of thy sin and that had been laid on thy back. See my hands, which have rightly been nailed to the tree for thy sake, because thou hadst wrongly stretched out thy hands to the tree. I slumbered on the Cross and the lance pierced my side for thy sake, who didst sleep in paradise and lettest out Eve from thy side. My side has healed the pain of thy side. And my sleep now leads thee out of the sleep of hell.

Arise then and let us go forth: from death to life, from corruption to incorruption, from darkness to eternal light. Arise, let us go forth from sorrow into joy, from the dungeon into Jerusalem that is above, from bonds to freedom, from prison to the happiness of Eden, from earth to heaven. My father is waiting for the lost sheep, an angel's throne is prepared, the servants stand waiting, the wedding chamber is ready, the eternal tabernacles and dwellings are open, the treasures of all good things are opened, the eternal Kingdom of Heaven is waiting for thee. . . ."[1]

This view of redemption must necessarily express itself in images, since it apprehends something that lies beyond death. At the same time this is suggested by the Bible itself, more accurately by the transition from the eschatology of the Old to that of the New Covenant. After being expelled from paradise, mankind as a whole cannot return to God unless a Redeemer comes from God himself. This saviour is prophesied in the Old Covenant for future times; and so on earth in transitory time, a ray of light and hope brightens the future. For the time being it is visible only to the Chosen People who is the bearer of the promises, and conceived as temporal. The fate of the dead as described in the Old Testament is characterized by its punitive aspect. The divine life that is given to the living in a form that is still one of promise does not yet penetrate into the depths of the grave. Faith, hope and love have their home in heaven; they cannot dwell where heaven is closed and the ruling reality is the *poena damni*, exclusion from the vision of God. It is of the essence of this penalty that it is *de jure* eternal, which is expressed by the fact that Hades is a place without hope, as the psalms and hymns state so emphatically.[2] That which lies beyond death is naturally not subject to time and change. In the Old Covenant death means having to leave the region of life and light, which are taken in an indivisibly natural-supernatural sense. Death is the same reality as seen by the apocalyptic seer: the Fourth Horseman

---

[1] Pseudo-Epiphanius, *Homily for Holy Saturday*, PG 43, 440-464. Other texts in Kroll, *God and Hell*. Bibl. Warburg, 1936.

[2] Cf. the hymn of Ezechias in the Good Friday Liturgy, Isaias 38. 10-20 in Lauds, and Psalm 87 in the Third Nocturn.

of the secret revelation is "death, followed by hell", the gate of hell
that introduces man into the lost region of Hades.

It is a shortcoming of Western theology that it does not consider seriously enough from what God has redeemed us. This
"from what", to which Eastern theologians gave their attention,
is nothing less than hell, the eternal exclusion from the presence of
God. True, the Old Testament world of promise belongs already
to the sphere of Redemption; but it is of decisive importance that
in this world of promise it is still possible to glance at what
mankind had by right incurred as the natural consequence of its
earthly existence such as it was lived. The *terminus a quo* of
Redemption is not a merely ideal possibility, it is the most real
actuality. Indeed it is so real that the Saviour in his vicarious
suffering had to descend into it in order to experience it from
within, and thus to be conformed to his brethren even in this.
Jesus is the last of the Old Testament saints that cry to God:
"Why hast thou forsaken me?" No one could utter this cry more
intensely than he whose life it is to be everlastingly generated by
the Father and, in this generation, to see the Father. Now he, too,
experiences what it means to lose God, to know him only as the
far-away Judge. The relationship by which Father and Son turn
towards each other in an eternal dialogue seems to be turned into
estrangement and indescribable loss, while, in the hour of darkness on the Cross, there is no light of hope and return at his
disposal. Even for the most just of the just there is the iron law
that in "the hour of God", "the day of God", which is the day of
judgment and wrath, the good things of the Father, the faith
that is experienced and felt, love and hope, are deposited with
God so as to remain inaccessible. The heavenly clothes are
stripped off, the heavenly images veiled. They all, Isaac, Job,
Jeremias, and lastly Jesus, walk naked and in extreme poverty and
humiliation through the door of darkness.

The reality of the *poena damni* is spiritual and can be experienced
only spiritually. This spiritual experience means passing through
the gate of hell. Beatitude will follow on Easter Day; on Holy
Saturday there is no reason to sing Alleluia. The descent of Jesus
into the reality of death that preceded Redemption is part of his
humiliations, even though this ultimate humiliation, beyond

which no other is possible, is already shot through with the light of Easter night, as for St John even the Cross itself. For this journey through Hades carries Redemption into it. This track through the trackless way makes an opening where before all had been completely closed. For this uttermost loneliness of death of him who has lost all connexion with the living, whose body lies fettered in its tomb and whose soul lets itself be bound with the bonds of the experience of Hades, introduces everything that is called communication and communion in the eternal sense. For this darkest of all dark nights of the soul sheds an eternal light where, without this vicarious night, there would have been only eternal darkness.

The Eastern Church has made this quite simple, elementary fact of faith the centre of its redemptive belief: that Jesus, walking through the kingdom of eternal death, has conquered and abolished it, substituting for it his own eternal life. Hence she celebrates Easter with a finality and exuberance unknown to the West. Instead, the West knows something that the spirituality of the East does not sufficiently recognize, namely the gifts of imitation which the Lord who descends into Hades gives to his Church. These are the Christian New Testament experiences of the dark nights. There are many of them, and the Church treasures them in her memory. Sometimes they become more widely known in the Church, but they rouse only a faint echo. And indeed, these nights are not meant to be known. They cannot be imitated; even the most stirring descriptions, like those of St John of the Cross, cannot give an adequate idea of what they are to those who have not experienced them, except for the knowledge that there are such descents into hell, as a Christian grace, that is as an imitation of Christ. Theologically it is no longer the same experience as that of the old prophets and saints when they felt themselves forsaken by God. But because the experience of Christ in the centre of time fulfilled and enveloped both the past and the future, the experience of the Christian is no less profound and intense. The man who prays, and who is called to experience that, for him, "God is dead", mostly knows no longer any hope. What is now will always be. Indeed, the "Now" can become so overpowering that it embraces also the past: what is now must always have been. The West treasures this experience of many saints like a precious relic. And it does not matter that those who experienced this have sometimes failed to interpret their sufferings in the full light of theology, seeing them in their humility usually only as a process of subjective purification. This may also be true. But the imitation of Holy Saturday is more important than that. Yet this can be begun only in ignorance, and involuntarily. Even as a vocation this experience leaves unperceived the communication with the Lord who leads the way. And thus its decisive effect, too, remains unknown to those who have it in this world; they know nothing of the share that, failing and powerless though they seemed to be, they may have contributed in order that the darkness of the world might be turned into light.

This turning point is the event of the reconciliation of the world, which can be expressed only as the perfect miracle of Easter night. He who was sealed in the tomb and in Sheol, through the power of heaven shares in the heavenly, eternal life. *Dux vitae mortuus regnat vivus.* Down to the late Middle Ages this happening (*Vorgang*) that can be expressed only as an event (*Ereignis*) has been celebrated in partly liturgical, partly dramatic, plays. In the Redentine Easter Play the church door, closed for the night, is the gate of hell at which Christ knocks, while the devils are holding discussions inside, and which he eventually bursts open with a great noise, to bring light into hell, which is now changed into the church. This is the correct Christian interpretation, and corresponds to that of the old sermon already cited.

In comparison with this, we see in Dante what happens if the Christian doctrine of redemption and eschatology is forced into the framework of the ancient cosmology. This had already begun with the Fathers and was developed in the medieval view of the world. An adequate presentation of this would need a separate study. It is enough for us to know that Dante's hell with its interior hierarchical structure, its order, logic and justice, is an essential piece of the created cosmos; it is a realm for sinners, yet carefully, one might almost say lovingly, designed by God. Yet there is not the slightest sign that Christ has ever been there; and we are bound to say that the man who traverses it under the guidance of a pagan sage is not walking in the footsteps of Christ.

The communication between the poet and sinners, which is re-established at every moment and again broken off without any consequences, has nothing to do with the communion which the advent of Christ has brought to this place of total loneliness. It is also self-contradictory, because there can be no real communion outside love, and love of the damned and for the damned cannot be made intelligible from the Christian point of view. Hence the most unintelligible feature for the Christian of today is the idea that a Christian can enter hell and leave it again just as he had entered it, while the only "event" that takes place during this journey is a solidarity that is confined to conversation and observation on the part of the traveller, and that is dissolved almost as soon as it is established. Charles Péguy's mockery that Dante had passed through hell as a tourist is objectively true. This kind of "hell" can be justified only in the sphere of imagination, not in a serious theology of revelation. It reflects not only the modification which the cosmological framework had imposed on revelation, but also the categories of personal consciousness that go with it. For, as we have said before, it was reserved to a later period to achieve this unity of personal consciousness that is necessarily at the same time also the consciousness of mankind. To the medieval mind some things were acceptable which were quite alien to the mind of the seventeenth century. It was due neither to particular cruelty nor to hardness, nor to special levity if the medieval prince kept his enemies chained, groaning and grinding their teeth in the darkest dungeons of his castle, over which men would dine and dance, but also work and pray, without having any difficulties of conscience. To ignore this leads to anachronisms—of which even Reinhold Schneider is guilty now and again. Dante belongs to his time, which is no longer ours. He could look at hell as one looks at an objective painting; though he is "in" it topographically, he does not share in its reality. The strange callousness which his poem shows in these parts—and not only in these—has nothing to do with the veiling of love in the "dark night of the soul".

Only in the Christian poetry of our own time do we find something that corresponds to the modern problem of lost man. It is sufficiently evident from the plays of Sartre what a "conversation" with the lost or between the lost (*Huis clos*) can be, even at its best: "discussion" in the literal sense of the word, that is "beating asunder". With hell, with Hades, no conversation is ultimately possible. If there is to be any communication at all— and from the Christian point of view it is possible only from the standpoint of the descent of Jesus Christ into the kingdom of the lost—then it is exclusively a dialectical one, in the form of participation or vicarious acceptance. It is an event that takes place in the most profound and solitary silence, incapable of being expressed dialogically, for its result cannot be proved to be visibly and intelligibly connected with its cause.

Paul Claudel's *Le repos du septième jour* is closest to Dante, and significantly placed in the pagan world of China. Here, too, we have a descent into hell, and in the darkness below there are discussions with the lost shades (this time it is the mother) and with the demon himself. But the descent of the Emperor is meant to be atoning and vicarious; he becomes a parable of Christ; when he again ascends, he is afflicted with leprosy and, as his Empire is now quiet, he departs into the mountains of contemplation. Charles Péguy dares to go even further, he whose main concern in every phase of his life was the solidarity of all mankind; who left the Church because he found it impossible to conceive hell, and who returned to it when he had understood the insufficiency of a merely earthly, socialist solidarity. As a socialist he wrote the first version of his *Jeanne d'Arc*, the tragedy of the solidarity of mankind; and after his return to Christianity he made of it his *Mystère de Jeanne d'Arc*. The socialist Jeanne cannot bear that her brethren should be "lost" and "damned"; she can begin her earthly mission only after she has consecrated herself even into communion with their damnation. In the end she receives this consecration as the price of the action she has accomplished, by being expelled from the communion of the saints in the Church and delivered over to the flames of hell in the night of the soul, dying for her brethren with the conviction that she herself is lost. The Christian Jeanne of the *Mystère* is shown only in her first decision, resolved *not to resign herself* to the loss of her brethren in the Christian sense. She knows in her prayer that she is rebelling against God. But without this rebellion, she says, even her Mass and her Communion become "worm-eaten and hollow". Madame Gervaise suggests that she should "resign herself to the will of God", but this cannot calm her. Only one last certainty saves her from this distress: she is sure in her revolt against the loss of her brethren to have touched unawares the inmost heart of God. God, too, is not neutral. God, too, does not "resign himself" to the incomprehensible, the intolerable, the impossible. At this point of the Christian writing of the West the East is seen to break through. The most French of all Frenchmen was yet a socialist, and though he did not introduce the doctrine and ideology of socialism into the Church, he brought to her that spark through which socialism has become an essential expression of the anthropological age.

Two poets have gone yet further in intimate association: Gertrud von le Fort, especially with her novel *The Last at the Scaffold*, and George Bernanos with all his novels and with the dramatization of Gertrud von le Fort's work in his *Dialogues des Carmélites*. The themes of the spiritual night, of vicarious suffering and communion penetrate each other. In Bernanos especially this happens always in view of the theme of absolute loss, which is shown not only in individual characters, such as the "Deceiver" or the heroine of *A Crime*, but also collectively in *Monsieur Ouine*. The poet is akin to Dostoievsky in that he experiences the surface of time as transparent, revealing final, eternal decisions and states. Only a thin veil need be drawn back to show heaven and hell as present. This explains the frightful seriousness of his writings on cultural politics, his urgent demands for earthly decisions: what is at stake is the soul and its salvation, Faust's pact with the Devil—Faust may here be France or the world. At the opposite pole to the despairing unbelievers who "search out the depths of Satan", this poet undertakes the Christian exploration of hell in spiritual communion with Claudel, Péguy and Léon Bloy. Dante's problem appears in a new form: the question whether communication is possible in a place which is by essence the breaking off of all communication. The solution can be found only in the following of Christ, for whom the contact with the place of absolute loneliness was established only by surrendering and losing the felt and lived contact in the Passion, in the passivity that was then only at the disposal of the will of the Father even unto death and the descent into the netherworld.

It is silly to blame these poets for burrowing in dark problems, to say that they would have done better to spread more Christian joy, more of the light of the Resurrection. Claudel and Péguy have done this abundantly; whereas Bernanos, in whose heart Christian joy was truly alive, could not tear himself away from the marvellous mystery of salvation, that the Light of grace and joy should have the power to give himself for the life of the world. And what do these Christian poets bring back from their journey through Hades if not "the mystery of the second virtue"? This is a Christian hope freed from its limitations which, seen in historical periods, has actually become (once more) possible when the cosmologization of hell such as Dante shows it was left behind and changed into an anthropological, that is to say interior, experimental understanding of what it means to be lost. As soon as this happened, the cry of forlornness on the Cross and the descent of the Redeemer, as well as the soteriological meaning of Christian com-passion became again, and more deeply, accessible.

One might say that the beginning of a spring of Christian hope is the mark of contemporary Christianity. The many theological studies on the subject that are being published indicate that here much still remains to be done for Christian thought. The more comprehensively this new beginning is interpreted the more correctly will it be understood. We are concerned with integrating the social feature of unity by which modern consciousness is characterized into the theological virtues, and especially into the structure of Christian hope. In this, as has been mentioned in the beginning, the respective shares of cosmic and historic evolution and of Christianity can hardly be apportioned quite accurately. They penetrate each other; the Christian factor in the consciousness of mankind was deepened and unified by different upheavals following each other, while the consciousness, thus enlarged, had yet first to be made capable of seeing the deepest Christian mysteries in their broadest scope.

This spring of hope has been canonized in the rose garden of Lisieux: there blooms the abyss of vicarious love. "God has given me his infinite mercy as my vocation; in this ineffable mirror

I contemplate his other properties. And thus they all appear to me radiant with love; his justice, too, perhaps even more than the others, seems to me enveloped in love. . . . If thy justice loves to be effective, though it extends only to this earth, how much more will thy merciful love long to inflame souls, as thy mercy extends to the heavens." The audacities of the little saint have not been surpassed by the poets, Péguy and Bernanos, who interpret her message.

Nor do they break down the barrier that confronts all *theologia viatorum* by turning the mystery of Christ's Cross and Sheol into something like an occult Gnostic system of salvation. The Church has erected a firm barrier against the old gnosis which threatened to overflow into the Church in the imprudent formulations of Origen. God's judgment is not in the hands of man, but in those of the one Jesus Christ to whom the Father has entrusted all judgment, because he humbled himself unto the death on the Cross. He, the Son of the Father, has known and personally experienced heaven, earth and the underworld in his redemptive way, therefore every knee must bow before him in heaven, on the earth and under the earth. His judgment will be the judgment of the Redeemer; yet it will not be a mere phantom judgment, but it will take place as the utterly serious mandate he has received from the Father, in the full truth of the "Day of the Lord". The fact that he judges us and does not abandon his judgment means that we belong to him in life and death, that he has power over our eternity, that, in his most just decision, he can place us on his right or left, can call us into his Kingdom or turn us away into the eternal fire. All fear and all hope tend towards him, the Redeemer and the Judge. All faith is directed towards his divine-human Person—not towards truths, states and conditions divorced from him—and living Christian faith necessarily involves a self-giving trust that recognizes the truth of him who reveals himself as the Redeemer and Judge even if understanding fails.

Consequently, the three theological virtues blend into that living indissoluble unity which is always theirs in the Holy Scriptures of the Old as well as of the New Covenant, whether the act of surrender be set in the light of triumphant love or in the night of Job and Jeremias. And surely such an act that is wholly bound up with the mystery of God's self-giving love must itself be enveloped in the radiance of mystery. It cannot be neatly resolved and rationally surveyed, but rather is full of blessed paradoxes for earthly reason that cannot keep step with its ever-increasing breadth. It is an act which, in its surrender, simply does not ask to know, but which, in the grace that is given to it, cannot refuse assent to the revelation received, and has to strive not to narrow it (*fides quaerens intellectum*—faith seeking understanding). Nevertheless, this act must always let itself be stripped bare by obedience, because living, loving and hoping faith is our form of following Christ and thus needs the form of the servant and humiliations in this life, so as to bear fruit unto eternal life. Thus the act remains truly open; it determines the judgment of the Lord neither to the one side nor to the other, nowhere establishing an *a priori* "impossibility" (that none of the brethren can be lost, or that some are certainly lost); and only in this way does it show itself as the act of genuine surrender, not only of reason and will, but of the whole person to the will of the Lord. And by thus sacrificing his existence the believer offers also that of his brethren. The act by which he does this is a social act within the Church, an act of communion just as much as a personal and individual act. But that this act should avail for those "in darkness and the shadow of death" is not due to the fact of the natural unity of mankind; it can only be found in the mystery of the mystical Body of the Saviour, so that every claim, every pious revolt (in the sense of Péguy's Jeanne d'Arc) has to be discarded in free surrender to the mystery. The co-redemptive efficacy of the faithful will attain its perfection only if each no longer wants anything for himself or for all, but simply says "Yes" to the redemptive will of God. "This is the victory which overcometh the world: our faith." (1 John 5. 4.)

Obviously, we are not concerned with re-interpreting or newly formulating either the act or the contents of faith. But its actual essence should become simple and transparent, it should be reborn and resurrected from the primeval sources of revelation; we would integrate into it those elements which it needs in order to attain its fullness, that is to say especially hope and love. This integration means at the same time that it will be stripped of all worldly accretions which can only distract and deflect from the divine nakedness of the Cross. This is not a means and a detour so as to attain to more profound mysteries. On the contrary, whatever insight is given to faith will enable it to entrust itself even more thoroughly and efficaciously to the supremely luminous darkness of the ever-greater divine love. Faith is offered no other solution of the torturing question of the loss of the brethren than that it should lose itself in the abyss of God. This is the only gesture by which man can be assimilated to the rhythm of these abysses and, through grace, learn to abandon himself completely to love.

D.   THE SACRAMENT OF THE BROTHER

MAN HAS transcended things; they can no longer be God for him. He has come to know himself sufficiently to have no more desire to worship himself. If then he is ready to acknowledge God, his relation to him becomes terrifyingly direct. There is really no zone left to be adored save God. Yet there is someone else, who is not God, and who has come nearer to him than ever before. This is his brother. In this mirror that is held ever before him, a thousand and a million times repeated, he has to look at himself whether he wants it or not. It is indeed an extremely realistic mirror that shows him all the variants of his qualities both good and bad, and those he most dislikes more clearly than the others. Man is bad-tempered with himself; and this malaise and nausea, provoked by being inescapably locked up with one's fellows, increases from Strindberg to Sartre and Simone de Beauvoir. This state should not be considered pathological, unless this term be taken literally as "word of a suffering", of man suffering from himself. In *Huis clos*, the extreme is reached that man must bear the unbearable because there is no escape. But why should he not for once honestly express his feelings: that he finds it unbearable to have to put up with himself, whether this himself be the "I" or the "thou", which, in fact, comes to the same—simply man with man?

Man must suffocate through man if, in this everlasting meeting with himself which makes up daily life, he meets no one else save man, no matter whether he meets himself in solitude or in community, in solitary community or in the crowds of traffic in the road or on the sports ground. Why should the "I" lose and offer it for a "thou" that, fundamentally, it cannot esteem any more than itself, if nothing else were offered in the "thou" than that which everyone knows, at least virtually, of himself? That means this being with its shut-in finiteness, terrified by ills which come when least expected: death and illness, insanity, interior and exterior catastrophes, a being that fear can inspire to astonishing achievements. The adventure of losing self will not be worthwhile if I do not meet God in my brother, if no breath of infinity stirs in this love, if I cannot love my brother with a love that comes from a higher source than my finite capacity of loving; in short, if what in our meeting may bear the sublime name of love does not come from God and return to him. For it will deliver a man neither from his prison nor from his solitude. Animals can love each other without knowing God, for they are not wholly conscious of themselves. But man's nature permits and demands this reflexion, and at a certain stage of his historical development he has known it so thoroughly that in it not only the individual, but the species as a whole, mankind, has seen itself in it; hence men can no longer love each other without God.

Perhaps the New Testament prophecy that the charity of many will grow cold envisages precisely our present time. It is a tragic epoch, for it must understand two things simultaneously: that nothing else is worthwhile in the world except man (because there is nothing else on which one can stake oneself)—and that yet ultimately man is not worthwhile. This is the time of philanthropism and perfected humanism, when all philosophies whether of the East or of the West centre on man. They are all concerned with the aid and development he should be given, and yet this interest has, whether openly or secretly, a bitterly cynical or a sweetishly insipid, or else an impersonal and inhuman flavour. There is no way out of this tragic situation, and man knows it himself. Somehow or other he feels he has been cheated in the prison of his nature, of his history and of his absurd planet. He looks for somebody who has defrauded him, but finds no one.

If, however, there were one who was truly man and at the same time God; a God who was not only infinite, unattainable majesty, but at the same time wholly man—such a one would give meaning to the world. Perhaps he came too soon. The Fathers of the Church and the medieval doctors took great pains to explain why he had come so late, at the "end of time". We ask: why did he not delay his coming till today, when life on earth has become unbearable without him? The reason probably is that the seed he sowed into the earth is breaking the soil and becoming visible only today, not only for the believers within the Church, who have always known it, but also for those outside, with an evidence striking as never before. The hour has come to the world when Christians and non-Christians are united in fraternal love as a question and a reality. Hence it is also the hour in which we must realize that, in its inmost being, Christian love transcends "Christianity" into the space of the world. Indeed, this transcending movement constitutes the essence of Christianity.

Christ's teaching on this is explicit: "For if you love them that love you, what reward shall you have? Do not even the publicans this? And if you salute your brethren only, what do you more? Do not also the heathens this? Be you therefore perfect, as also your heavenly Father is perfect." (Matt. 5. 46-48.) There is the close finite circle of marriage, friendship, the nation and even— the Church. And a certain (much too narrow) view of Christianity could suggest that Christian love is primarily the love of Christians for one another. For we read in St John that the world is to recognize Christian doctrine from this mutual love of Christians in the world. The whole first Epistle of St John treats of this love between Christians that is God's life in the world. St Paul, too, often describes the Church as that "body" of Christ which is built up from the mutual love of its members, while recommending Christians to live in peace with those outside as far as possible. If this were the central aspect, it might warrant the view that the sphere of mutual love within the Church is the luminous centre of mankind, and that those outside it are to be urged, perhaps even compelled, to enter it so that they may also participate in the grace of mutual love.

Such a perspective, while not actually false, fails to realize on what

Christian love is based. This love means going forth to those out-side, those who love not, to the lost brother, to the enemy. When we were still enemies Christ loved us and died for us. (Rom. 5. 8.) This is the foundation of Christianity, and cannot be neglected by the love that follows Christ. The man who is farthest away is the one whom Christ calls the nearest, the "neighbour". In his description of the Last Judgment (Matt. 25) he tells us that behind this "farthest", the man who hungers and is thirsty, behind the naked, the sick, the prisoner, he stands himself, hidden but intended, unfelt yet truly touched. If this is so, then this neighbour whom he came to seek, to love, to bring home by the sacrifice of his life, was for him already more than merely a lost man. Love can only love itself. God's love can only love God, even in the world and in all that is lost. If the Son goes out to bring back his enemy and to give him the love that he has not, he must see God behind him and in him. For God the Father created this man, formed him to be his image and likeness, loved and called him and gave him an indelible sign, the sign of belonging to the Son, to the Word, to Redemption and the Church. Therefore, the Son, the Light goes into the darkness of the world that does not receive and understand him, he enters an alien sphere. And through this outgoing he comes into the sphere of the Father: for the lost world is his Father's holy creation. Hell, too, is the sphere of the Father: he is the judging God, the keeper of his own sacred world order. While the Son goes out into these spheres he remains at the same time in the will of the Father who wills to surrender him for the world, who sends him into the work of Redemption. Consequently, he must also see the Father in the brother who has become a stranger, and go to him accompanied by the will of the Father which is effective through the Holy Spirit.

Since the Father created all things in the Son, he allowed the darkness and estrangement of sinners only because he foresaw the future journey of his Son; in the intention of the Father all strange-ness remains within this love of the Son that is never estranged and which yet, to remain within the inmost will of the Father, has to pass over into the darkness, into the world of hatred and loss. In Christian love as it was originally, the love of the enemy was the beginning of the Church's love. Or, expressed differently: the love of the Church, indeed, the Church as such, essentially passes beyond itself to the world, which, on this account, is itself potential Church, and so a sphere of the sacred. The Church is not estranged from God, for it simply follows in the footsteps of Jesus, just as he walked in the world of darkness in the way of the Father's will and work. Coming from the Father and tending towards the Son, hence overshadowed by the Holy Spirit, the whole of creation, however estranged from God its behaviour may be, is from the beginning a sacred sphere, and so one that belongs to the Church. Being, therefore, in principle her dwelling, it must also itself be made as inhabitable as possible.

The Gospel shows that Christ at first intended to announce and found, not a Church separate from the world, but the "kingdom of God". In the primary idea of the Redemption, this kingdom would have been light and life flowing from God immediately into the world. It would have been wholly interior, and in it the whole law would have been fulfilled. Humanly, but not incorrectly speaking, the structural Church is only a secondary plan of Redemption, which had become necessary because men, that is the Chosen People, did not receive and accomplish Redemption as pure *metanoia*, as a conversion from the inmost heart.[1] But this does not prevent the "foundation" of Jesus with its hierarchy, its Sacraments and manifold institutions from being still the Kingdom open to the world. The love of Jesus, which gives itself for all sinners, is itself this kingdom. It is not a mutual human love ("Do not also the heathens this?"), but the love that, surrendering itself to non-love, experiences the Father's love beyond death in the grace of the resurrection. The mutual love within the Church which Paul and John praised so exultantly is yet, radically understood, always a love that helps fundamentally to build up the Church itself; this means it has its roots in the sphere where Jesus founds the Kingdom of God as a whole. His saying that he is behind each of the poorest and of those in need of love is the *Magna Charta* of his love. This means he is not even a little *more* present in the Christian than in the stranger who perhaps does not know him at all, and who precisely for this reason is all the

[1] Guardini, *The Lord*, London, 1956.

poorer and more needy, hence all the more the Sacrament of Jesus Christ. This stranger is always the primary "object" of love, while the love within the Church is rather the sacred *sign* of the love that passes over into the world. Of itself it does not stop short at the frontier of the Church, indeed, being love, it does not know this frontier at all. It is its essence to transcend it and *thus* to reveal the essence of the Church herself. For transcending love is never private, it is always the love of the Church, drawn directly from the love of Jesus Christ that he has given his bride for her property which she is to administer and pass on. In so far as the lover comes *from* God, he comes also from Christ and from the Church. God, Christ and the Church form an inseparable whole in which love has its source.

Not only its source but also its motive. This may be a scandal to the brother who cannot believe in God, Christ and the Church. He is loved ultimately for God's sake. This is the God who is love from all eternity and needs no creature; who has revealed himself in time in Jesus Christ, his Son, and who has created the Church which makes visible something of the reality of Jesus Christ and thus of the reality of the Kingdom of God in Heaven. Love must not stop short at man, however miserable and in need of love he may be, and this distinguishes Christian love from every form of humanitarianism. It loves God through the brother, God in himself, and God for us in Christ and in the Church. It must do this, because love, coming from God, is infinite and must therefore reach back to God himself. Such love is possible, because the created person who is loved is grasped in his true reality only in relation to God; for he comes from God and goes to God; he is created, called and redeemed by God, and his special vocation is given him by God's grace. Here we have to recall that God, the sea and abyss of Being, is not a being among others, hence not an "object" that might be detached from a surrounding world, and especially not from the knowing subject. He is, as Nicholas of Cusa used to say, the non-other, *non aliud*. He cannot be this, precisely *because* he, being absolute Being, is superior to all that is relative. Anything finite can only be loved as open towards this Absolute, not otherwise. Else the act in which it is embraced is not love, but concupiscence closing in upon it, nor is the object really loved, because all that makes it truly lovable comes from its open relation to eternal love and its glory.

The lover need not know this at all: neither that his own love, which he will hardly esteem very highly, comes from another region, nor that God is behind the being he loves, whom he has perhaps picked up on the road between Jerusalem and Jericho. If you understand, it is not God. For in this parable of the Last Judgment not only the wicked, who have not loved, are disconcerted, but also the good: "When did we see thee hungry and fed thee, thirsty and gave thee drink?" (Matt. 25. 37). Since God is incomprehensible, Christ, too, in whom God appeared, and the Church, the Body of Christ, are hidden in mystery; hence it is not necessary, indeed not even possible, that Christian love should understand whence it comes and whither it goes. For this reason it is given us by Christ as a *commandment*, which we are to practise in obedience and faith, and to this obedience promises are attached. These are that the love we practise *really* comes from God and goes to him, that it really reveals God in the world, and that in it men are able to recognize the truth of the revelation of God in Christ. If even the lover is incapable of recognizing the relation between the man he loves and the God that is hidden in him, how could this be done by the loved one? If the latter is scandalized by Christian love, surely this is irrelevant and cannot cause it to waver. For charity is not asked to discover Christ "behind" the brother, "representing" him in a kind of hide and seek game, still less to love Christ "in the place of" the brother, so that there would be an indistinct to and fro between the two subjects. It suffices for him to love the brother together with Christ; then he will love him with a love that ascends towards the Father, seeing, too, through the hidden and disfigured face of the brother the original of all this disfigurement—for love. Why should there be such remoteness, such inaccessibility among men with its consequent despair and abjection? Why has the Creator allowed this? Where is this incomprehensible state of affairs justified, conquered and appeased? Surely nowhere but in the Son, who has been the surety of the goodness of creation from the beginning of the world, and who has resolved all our distance and despair. So there is in the distant, inaccessible brother not only the image, but the reality of the divine love that suffers for him, and the more remote he is, the clearer and stronger will it shine.

To love the brother for God is demanded the more insistently, as human, even Christian love can in no way be compared with the redeeming love of Christ. Christian love is no match for the "No" of sin that opposes it. Nor can it appropriate God's greater power like an instrument with which to force the alien lock. Its armour or light is but prayer, surrender and self-offering, and in addition hope that springs from faith, which is perhaps its most powerful weapon. "Love believes all, hopes all." "The love and faith which you have to God and to all the saints." (Philem. 5.) Love always hopes in God. It places the other within the transcendent greatness and openness of God, which can change him above himself into the being that love expects him to become. In this hope love itself can receive mysterious awakening powers which co-operate in the upward flight of the brother, powers which, from the original image that it discovers and calls forth in him, make it appear to be creative force itself. Yet love will never attribute this power to itself. It hopes in God and in the brother, who can listen to the voice of God; and, hoping, it rouses hope in the brother.

Certainly this hope is directed towards the love of the brother. But the love of the brother is God's love in him, which he lovingly understands, and allows to work in him. To recognize this love means to recognize, consciously or unconsciously, that the love of God has taken the form of man. It means recognizing Jesus Christ, whether his existence be known or not. For I acknowledge him simply by admitting that God's love—really the love of *God* —puts me, as a man, under an obligation. If a man does this he is, openly or in a hidden way, a member of the Church in so far as she is the community of the saints built up by fraternal love. If a person has hope for his brother, he hopes that his brother may find God, Christ and the Church. Nothing else would be worth wishing for the brother in charity.

In this sense not only God and Christ, but the Church, too, is ever the goal and "object" of love, it is that for the sake of which even the man who is farthest away will be loved. It is true, on the one hand, that love does not stop short at the church door, but flows through the Church, unbroken and unweakened, over into the world. St Augustine says: "Extend your love to all the parts of the earth, if you want to love Christ truly, for the members of Christ are spread throughout the whole world. If you love a part you are divided, you are not in the whole body, not under its Head."[1] Nevertheless, it is equally true that the individual is loved only in view of the whole, in which he shares in different degrees and stages, either as an incorporated living member of the "Body" or as a dead member, if he is a sinner, or only as a possible member, if he has not yet attained to faith in Christ.[2]

But the fact that the individual is loved in view of the whole does not invalidate the concrete situation. In this, Christian love differs from pure humanitarianism. The situation is the meeting with the brother, who becomes here and now my neighbour. We misuse this precious word if we give it the same extension as the term brother. All men are brethren; as Christians they are so in a stricter sense. Christ says: "You are all brothers." But my neighbour can always only be one. Hence, though there is a universal brotherly love, there is no universal love of my neighbour, but always only a particular one. For the Christian this is due to the fact that Christ can never be for him the universal, but always the unique Person that meets him with an absolute claim, that turns the brother into his neighbour. This singles him out from the crowd of those who may possibly have to be loved, making him the one who demands just now to be loved irrevocably. Thus he becomes the bearer of God's call, the Sacrament of the word of God as it comes to me. This Sacrament is dispensed in daily life, not in the church; in conversation, not during a sermon. It is administered not in prayer and meditation, but in situations where prayer shows that it is genuine and where meditation results in the apostolate. There it will be decided whether I have really heard God's word in my prayer, whether I have received his Body and Blood in church effectively. And the decision is made in the right way, if it is evident that I am

[1] John tr. 10, n. 3; PL 35, 2060.
[2] Thomas, 3 Sent. d. 13. q. 2, a. 2, sol. 2.

willing to give my neighbour the bread and wine of the word and
of my own life.

Because Jesus as a whole is wholly pure, therefore his whole
Flesh is food and his whole Blood is drink. For all his works are
holy and all his words are true. Therefore his Flesh is food
indeed and his Blood is drink indeed. For he nourishes and
restores all mankind with the Flesh and Blood of his Word as
with a pure food and a pure drink. In the second place, after
his Flesh, Peter and Paul and all the apostles are also a pure
food; and in the third place their disciples. And thus every man
is capable of becoming a pure food for his neighbour according
to his worthiness and the purity of his intention. If a man is
unable to hear this he may pervert it and turn away his ear as
those who said: "How can this man give us his flesh to eat?
Who can hear it? And they left him." You, however, if you
are sons of the Church and the Word made flesh is living among
you, will realize what we are saying. For these are mysteries of
the Lord: every man has a certain food in himself; and if it is
good and he draws from it and "from the treasure of his heart
brings forth good things", he offers pure food to his neighbour.
If the law of God which the Church preaches is thus understood
it will be above all human laws and will be believed in truth
to be God's law.[1]

The lover is the "Church". He does not dispense his love
sovereignly, but serving, not as the head, but as a member. Thus,
and only thus, will he do so really in a humility that does not
"master the situation" and is "a match for it"; but he will in
this situation do something that he cannot overlook, giving
something that is necessarily more than himself, even though this
"more" may demand staking his whole self on it. Only then will
the giver not be superior, nor the poor brother who receives be
humiliated by the lover. He will be humiliated only in this that
he is a sign of the love of God humiliating itself, and the lover
will be this for the same reason. Love is possible only between
humiliated human beings; else the gentle sacrament of which
Origen spoke will turn at once into a savage devouring of each
other, as in Kleist's *Penthesilea*. What is humiliating is above all

[1]Origen, hom. 7 in *Lev.*, Baehrens 6, 386–388.

this, that the event on which everything depends, the love expressed in this situation, has nothing mystical about it and bears no religious emphasis. It may happen occasionally that such an event is marked by something like lightning flashing from heaven and forcing both partners to go down on their knees for a moment. But mostly nothing tangible will happen, nothing except this tiny, hardly noticeable movement towards each other, this turning, somewhere perhaps beyond all words and experiences, so that it cannot even be actually perceived, but is realized only from the consequences. For from now on word and life will spring from a love that had not been there before, but has suddenly and incomprehensibly come forth. The event is hidden in the profane world, as the word of God, too, is a wholly hidden word that addresses me through the brother, demanding now, here, at once and inescapably, the service of love. And yet it is not simply a mere word of nature; the words of nature are general and may become so hackneyed, as has happened in our time, that they have hardly any meaning for us. Why should a man who does not esteem himself in the depth of his being esteem his equals? Why should he expect his brother to be more high-minded than he is himself? Why should he not seek to establish the communication on the plane where he himself is at home, that is in sin, turned away from God? No, there is something else in the apparently "natural" situations that is a call. This call is continuous, but it is embodied, it has taken flesh in the everyday situation.

Living means being spoken to; we need only be there to listen. Every one of us is wearing a coat of mail of which we soon fail to be aware because we are so used to it. But there are moments when it is pierced and the soul is stirred to receptivity. The signs of being addressed are nothing extraordinary, something outside the normal order of things. They are just what happens, what happens in any case; the "address" adds nothing to them. The waves of the ether are always in motion, but we have mostly turned off our receiver. Everything that happens is cosmic happening, by which I am addressed. Only by sterilizing it and depriving it of its address can I regard what happens to me as part of the events of the world that do not concern me. The interconnected, sterilized system into which all this need only be integrated is the titanic work of mankind. Its signs have this characteristic that they are to be found in a dictionary, though this need not be written down. And however secretly this is transmitted, whoever looks for these signs knows how to interpret them; he knows what term of life this or that sign means; it can be "looked up". The common signature of all these doings is their universality; they remain the same, what has been found out is always valid, the rules, laws and analogies may always be applied. Real faith—if I may thus call the listening—begins where the looking-up ends, where one would not dream of it. What happens to me says something to me; but no secret knowledge can tell me what it is that it says to me, for it has never been said before, and it is not composed of sounds that have been uttered before. It looks at me in terrifying uniqueness.[1]

Speaking from the Christian point of view, it is the work of the Holy Spirit that this Word of God—which once had to sound loud and audible for all who wanted to hear in the midst of history—should be hidden in the everyday situation in the world. Once the Spirit rested only on Jesus, who, returning to the Father and as a sign that he the Redeemer had come back to the Creator, poured it forth over the world and over the Church, who is his Bride only in the transcendence of love. And as the Spirit calls the world to the Church, so he also calls the Church to the world. When the Church goes out, the world comes home. Thus, in the parable of the Good Shepherd the shepherd is outside: "He calleth his own sheep by name and leadeth them out. And when he hath let out his own sheep, he goeth before them: and the sheep follow him, because they know his voice." Here the movement goes unequivocally from the inner room (the "Church") into the world and everyday life, where the voice sounds and the Shepherd goes before. He does so in so far as he is a good shepherd: "The good shepherd giveth his life for his sheep. . . . No man taketh it away from me. . . . And I have power to lay it down: and I have power to take it up again. This commandment have I received from the Father." Going out, giving his life: going out from the Father, returning

[1] Martin Buber, *Zwiesprache*, 1947, 145-148.

to the Father, going out and going in finally becomes the same movement. Thus the flock, too, is within and without: "And other sheep I have that are not of this fold: them also must I bring." And he does not say that outside his voice cannot be heard: on the contrary: "They shall hear my voice: and they shall be one fold and one shepherd." Thus this Man who goes in and goes out becomes the door that opens in both directions, and the opening of this door is Redemption: "I am the door. By me, if any man enter in, he shall be saved: and he shall go in and go out and shall find pastures." (John 10. 1-18.) The opposition between what is profane and what is sacred is indeed fully justified in its place, else there could be no movement. Yet in this openness and this reciprocally flowing movement the opposition is transcended by the unity of him in whom and for whom all things have been created, and who has therefore been charged by the Father to bring them home.

Nevertheless, a man will find God in all worldly things and especially in his brother who becomes his neighbour only if he is willing to seek and find God also in himself, in the sanctuary of prayer and the Word and Sacrament of the Church. The cosmos becomes sacred through the holiness of the Church, and the Church has not so much to make propaganda in the world, but above all to pray and to remain in charity. Christ has commanded us to withdraw into our inner chamber so as to remain before the Father who sees in secret, he has advised us to sell our belongings so as freely to follow him, to give up marriage in order to be undivided and pleasing to God alone, even to leave our own will to take his will for ours in all things. All this remains the foundation of the Christian apostolate in the world, which can never be abrogated. Those who are called out of the world must really come from within, else they could not show the way to anyone. And yet, if we consider the Scriptural message as a whole, how far removed this is from any other religious call to enter into oneself! How open it is to the world, and how unprotected the life of the faithful: like sheep among the wolves! How little fear there is for the fate of the "little flock" that is to come, to whom are prophesied the same persecutions of irreconcilable hatred, and for whom there is no other defence than that he will remain with them always until the end of the world. For they are set on his way to go "where they would not" and where grace draws them, to give their soul for their brethren beyond their own will or resistance.

All the aspects under which we have reviewed Christianity have broadened its meaning. Truths were disclosed which had been hidden in it, generally known already but not fully developed, which had been half-forgotten or neglected. Today mankind is entering new stages of its development, asking new questions that have never been heard in this way before. Whether Christianity is able to make God's answer to them credible will depend on how deeply Christians understand, live and love their own truth, on the ardour with which they let themselves be seized by the Spirit which is a spirit of eternal youth. It will depend on how courageously they dare to confront the mystery of this hour of the world, supported by the mystery of the Church. And success (if this word is here suitable at all) cannot be hoped for from surveyable syntheses between Church and world, for such have not been promised, least of all for our own age. This unity remains an eschatological concept. But the salvation of both will be in the most vital meeting, which for the Church will ever mean struggle and persecution.

The priest and the Levite who went past without "meeting" knew nothing of God's being and will, though they were experts on God. We are not told whether the Samaritan was a devout believer. He knows only as much as he does: "No man hath seen God at any time. If we love one another, God abideth in us, and charity is perfected in us." (1 John 4. 12.)